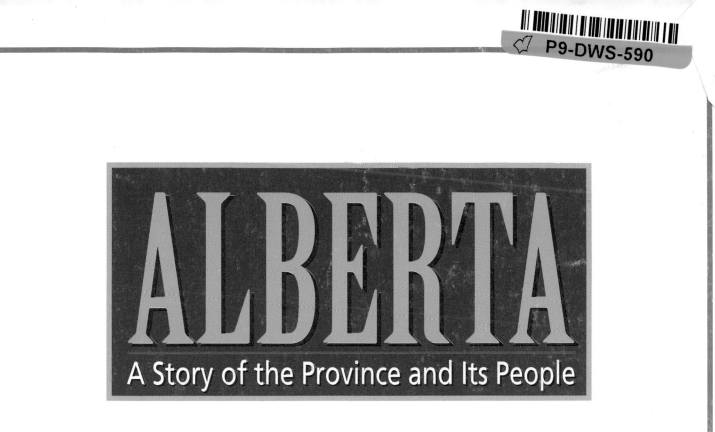

ALBERTA
A Story of the Province and Its People

by MARSHALL
JAMIESON

REIDMORE BOOKS
Edmonton, Alberta, Canada

Reidmore Books wishes to thank the following people for their insights and support in the development of this textbook:

Teaching Consultants
Maureen Duguay
St. Brendan Elementary School
Edmonton, Alberta

Marion Berry
St. Boniface School
Edmonton, Alberta

Historical Researcher
Stanley Gordon
Edmonton, Alberta

Canadian Cataloguing in Publication Data

Jamieson, Marshall, 1943-
    Alberta

    Includes index.
    ISBN 1-895073-62-6

    1. Alberta—History—Juvenile literature.
2. Indians of North America—Alberta—History—
Juvenile literature. I. Title.
FC3661.2.J34 1992   971.23   C93-091009-5

THOMSON
NELSON

1120 Birchmount Road
Scarborough, Ontario
M1K 5G4
(416) 752-9100

Printed and bound in Canada
2 3 4 5 05 04 03 02

Credits

Editorial: Leah-Ann Lymer, Carolyn Pogue-Phipps, James Manis, Jennifer Keane, Boomer Stralak
Illustrations: Yu Chao & Wang Jue
Maps: Wendy Johnson, Johnson Cartographics, Edmonton, AB
Design & Typesetting: Pièce de Résistance Ltée., Edmonton, AB
Printing: Quality Color Press

Excerpts and Adaptations

11 Excerpted with permission from *My Tribe, the Crees* by Joseph Dion (Glenbow 1979)
20 Excerpted from W. Kaye Lamb, ed., *Journals and Letters of Alexander Mackenzie* (London, Eng: Cambridge 1970)
41 Excerpted from William Czumen, *Recollections About the Life of the First Ukrainian Settlers in Canada* (Edmonton: Canadian Institute of Ukrainian Studies, 1989)
41 Excerpted from *Papers of W.J. Sisler*, Manitoba Provincial Archives
42 Adapted from Sarah Ellen Roberts, *Of Us and the Oxen* (Saskatoon: Modern Press, 1968)
44 Excerpted from Frank Gilbert Roe, *Getting the Know-How* (Edmonton: NeWest Press, 1982)
44 Saskatchewan Provincial Archives
45 Excerpted from *Papers of W.J. Sisler*, Manitoba Provincial Archives
46 Excerpted from an interview with Eric Lloyd, The Glenbow Archives, Calgary
47 Adapted from *Alberta Historical Review*, Vol 21, No 4, 1973 (Calgary: Alberta Historical Society)
54 Stephan Stephansson, "Toast to Alberta"
68, 69, 70, 71 Excerpted from Doug Owram, ed., *The Formation of Alberta* (Calgary: Historical Society of Alberta, 1979)
82 Excerpted from T.D. Regehr, *The Possibilities of Canada are Truly Great: The Autobiography of Martin Nordegg* (Toronto: Macmillan, 1971)
84, 98 Excerpted from Warren Caragata, *Alberta Labour: A History Untold* (Toronto: Lorimer, 1979)
99 Excerpted from James Gray, *The Winter Years* (Toronto: Macmillan, 1976)
100 Excerpted from Jean Burnet, *Next-Year Country* (Toronto: University of Toronto Press, 1951)
101 Excerpted from L.M. Granger and Michael Bliss, *The Wretched of Canada* (University of New Brunswick Press and University of Toronto Press)
108 Excerpted from Joy Kogawa, *Obasan* (Toronto: Lester & Orpen Dennys, 1981)

Photo Credits

Photos are credited as follows: T=Top, B=Bottom, L=Left, R=Right.
NAC = National Archives of Canada
PAA = Provincial Archives of Alberta

7   PAA / Harry Pollard Collection / P 467
13 PAA / Harry Pollard Collection / P 129
14 PAA / Harry Pollard Collection / P 467
19 NAC / C1348
20 NAC / C 2771
22 NAC / PA 9240
26 The Glenbow Archives / NA 1237-1
34 PAA / Archives Collection / A 2571
35 Calgary Stampede / Jack Dillon Collection
36 PAA / Ernest Brown Collection / B 113
37 The Glenbow Archives
39 PAA / Archives Collection / A 7537
40 Canadian Pacific Archives
41 NAC / C 15020
43 PAA / Archives Collection / A 2446
45 NAC / C 17574
53 T- PAA / Archives Collection / A 2096
    B- PAA / OMI (Oblate) Collection / Ob 3161
55 PAA / Archives Collection / A 5007
56 The Glenbow Archives / NA 1752 44
57 PAA / Archives Collection / A 7383
58 The Glenbow Archives / NA 2923 -1
59 PAA / Ernest Brown Collection / B 7232
60 The Glenbow Archives / NA 3091 30
62 PAA / Archives Collection / A11 210
68 PAA / Ernest Brown Collection / B 6656
69 PAA / Archives Collection / A 1188
70 PAA / Public Affairs Bureau Collection / PA 3670
71 PAA / Ernest Brown Collection / B 6596
72 PAA / Archives Collection / A 439
73 NAC / PA 1305
74 PAA / Archives Collection / A 3355
80 PAA / Ernest Brown Collection / B 3152
81 PAA / Archives Collection / A 8141
83 NAC / PA 21617
85 PAA / Archives Collection / A 1775
86 PAA / Harry Pollard Collection / P 1301
88 PAA / Archives Collection / A 2171
89 PAA / Ernest Brown Collection / B 5683
94 PAA / Archives Collection / A 482
96 PAA / Archives Collection / A 3973
98 PAA / Archives Collection / A 2916
99 PAA / Archives Collection / A 5145
100 PAA / Archives Collection / A 3742
102 PAA / Archives Collection / A 1797
107 NAC / PA 137014

Front Cover
Clockwise from top: NAC, NAC, PAA, PAA, Glenbow Archives

Back Cover
PAA

We have made every effort to correctly identify and credit the sources of all photographs, illustrations, and information used in this textbook. Reidmore Books appreciates any further information or corrections; acknowledgement will be given in subsequent editions.

CONTENTS

Why Study History?

The study of **history** is the study of past time. History tells what happened in the past. All groups of people tell stories about the past. For example, families tell stories about what happened to their members in the past.

Facts and Dates

Facts and *dates* are the building blocks of the study of history. Learning to use facts and dates is a skill, like learning how to multiply or how to spell.

A fact is what happened. A date is when it happened. The following are a few dates and facts from Alberta's history:

1. Alberta became a province on September 1, 1905.
2. Twenty-one people were killed in the Cypress Hills Massacre in 1873.
3. The railway arrived in Calgary in the summer of 1883.

If the study of history was nothing more than collecting facts and dates, it would soon get boring. An **historian** is really interested in why something happened, what people did, and how the event made the world different.

For example, fact number 1 says Alberta became a province in 1905. It became a province for a reason. In 1880 there were few settlers in Alberta. In 1901 the population was much larger. Still, the prime minister of Canada at that time did not believe Alberta should become a province yet. Why did he change his mind? How did the lives of the people change when Alberta became a province?

Fact number 2 shows us how a simple fact becomes complicated when we look at it closely. In 1873, 20 Native people and one white man were killed. The white men told one version of what happened. The only Native **witness** was a young boy who escaped.

This one event tells us about the people who lived at that time. It also explains why Canada sent the North-West Mounted Police to Alberta.

Fact number 3 also has some hidden meanings. A railway is just steel rails and steam engines. How could it turn a tiny fur trading post into a big city? Who built the railway and why? What effect did the railway have on the rest of Alberta? You will learn answers to these questions in this book.

Like a detective, an historian tries to sort out what happened and who made it happen. Dates help the historian understand how one event might have led to another.

CHANGE

People think, make their living, vote, and eat differently today than they did 50 years ago. A difficult question to answer is why do things change. For example, why did most people live on farms 100 years ago, while today they live in cities?

History helps us to understand how things changed in the past. There are few places that have changed as quickly as Alberta. In this book, you will read about the people and events of Alberta's past.

How Is This Book Organized?

There are many special features in this book to help you with your study of Alberta. Each chapter begins with a **Timeline** to help you identify important dates and facts. A **Chapter Focus** features four cartoon students, who will ask questions. Their questions will help you organize your thoughts as you read.

You will find many stories about Albertans in this book. **Sidebars** give you more information about people, events, or things. **In Their Own Words** sections tell stories in the actual words of people who lived in Alberta's past. These will help you to "hear" what happened to some Albertans.

Discussing the Issues sections will help you to talk about issues in Alberta's past.

New words are **boldfaced** within the text. You will find their definitions in the **Glossary** at the back of the book. Difficult words in the **In Their Own Words** passages are defined at the end of the section.

You will also find an **Index** at the end of the book. The **Index** will help you to find certain people, places, events, things, and subjects in the book.

Question Boxes

Every chapter also has a number of boxes which include questions and activities.

UNDERSTANDING THE STORY

You will find this question box near an **In Their Own Words** section. The questions in this box will help you to think about the story you have just read.

READING MAPS

The maps in this book give information about the land of Alberta. For example, they show the location of places, such as towns and cities. Refer to the maps many times as you read the text. The questions in the "Reading Maps" boxes will help you to understand the maps.

READING PICTURES

Pictures show us the way things looked in the past. This question box will appear near some pictures. The questions will help you uncover information about the past.

UNDERSTANDING THE PEOPLE

History is made by people. The history of Alberta is full of interesting characters who played a part in our story. This question box asks you to think about particular people in Alberta's history. Try to ask similar questions about all the people you read about in this book.

GATHERING INFORMATION

You will find this question box at the end of each chapter. The questions help you to review and think about what you have learned in the chapter.

FURTHER STUDY

You will also find this question box at the end of each chapter. The questions and activities will ask you to use other books and resources to find more information about Alberta.

6000 BC *The first people appear in Alberta*

1717 *Europeans first enter the Chipewyan land*

1870 *Canada takes control of the Northwest*

1877 *Blackfoot, Peigan, Blood, and Sarcee sign Treaty Number 7*

1899 *Cree, Beaver, Chipewyan, and Slavey Natives give northern Alberta to the Canadian government in Treaty Number 8*

CHAPTER FOCUS

Who were the first Albertans? Archaeologists believe that Native people lived in what is now Alberta at least 12 000 years ago. In this chapter, you will learn about the many groups of Natives who lived—and still live—in Alberta.

Where did the Native people come from? Who were they?

Did you know that my people lived in Alberta for thousands of years before any Europeans or Asians arrived?

What was Native life like before the Europeans came?

How did the lives of Native people change when they met the Europeans?

CHAPTER 1

THE NATIVE PEOPLE OF ALBERTA:

As Long as the Grass Shall Grow

In 1992 many North Americans celebrated the voyage of Christopher Columbus. He had sailed from Spain to America 500 years before. Many Native people, however, laugh at the idea that Columbus "discovered" America.

"How could he discover something," they asked, "when we knew it was there all the time!" In fact Native people have lived in North America for many thousands of years. But where did they come from?

ORIGINS: Who Were the First People?

Many **myths** passed on from **generation** to generation among the Native people tell the story that the people were created here in America. A Blackfoot myth tells how Napi, or Old Man, created the world, the people, and all the animals.

Archaeologists have a different version of how the people came to America. They describe a **scene** long ago in northern Canada. A small group of hunters follow a huge beast called a **woolly mammoth**. They kill it with spears tipped with stone. The hunters carry the meat to a cave on a rocky ridge above the Bluefish River.

The first people may have come to North America following the woolly mammoth and other animals. How do you think the first people hunted the mammoth?

A few years ago, an archaeologist discovered that cave, along with piles of bones and some tools. He wondered about the people who lived there. Who were they? Where did they come from? Scientific tests show that the bones in that cave are about 25 000 years old.

From Asia to North America

Archaeologists believe that the people of Bluefish River came from **Asia** because similar tools and animal bones were found there. How did they cross the water that today separates Asia and America? Another group of scientists called **geologists** tell us that about 25 000 years ago, much of North America was covered in ice. The water level of the ocean was lower and land connected Asia and North America.

The first people could have crossed this land bridge from Asia. They were hunters following their prey: woolly mammoths, giant bison, bears, and moose. They killed these large animals with spears tipped with stone

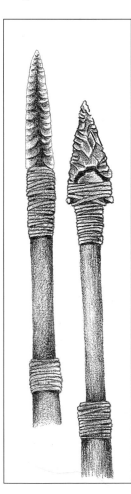

points, as sharp as razor blades.

Many archaeologists believe that these hunting families were the **ancestors** of all the North American Natives. As the ice melted, the animals moved south and the people followed. The first people reached what is now Alberta at least 12 000 years ago.

When the mammoths became extinct, the

The early Native people hunted with stone-tipped spears. The stone edges were as sharp as razors. How do you think the hunters made the tips?

*For thousands of years the early people drove bison over **buffalo jumps**. Study this picture. How do you think these people drove the animals off the cliffs?*

people hunted the bison, or buffalo as it is often called. The hunters killed the bison by **stampeding** them over the edges of cliffs. The Head-Smashed-In Buffalo Jump site in southern Alberta was used for this.

The early people travelled on foot. Their dogs carried many of their belongings. Although they did not have metal, they made very good use of stone. They used stones to hold down their **tipis**, and hot stones to heat water. They used stone tips for knives and spears. They made these blades sharp by chipping their edges with a stone tool.

The people also used stones to build **monuments** in the shapes of animals. All across the **plains** they marked their sacred spaces with circles of stone. The circles are called **medicine wheels**.

Two Ways of Life

Native people have lived in Alberta for about 12 000 years. They developed two quite different ways of life, based on the land in which they lived. Some lived on the plains and others in the **woodlands** (forests).

The lands of the people were not marked off with **boundaries** like the provinces and countries of today. The Native people roamed over huge distances. They lived in one area during one season and perhaps moved to another area for another season. Some people, such as the Cree, moved back and forth between the plains and the woodlands.

The People of the Plains

The Plains people lived a life close to nature. They created a rich life of the imagination, with stories, legends, and myths full of wisdom handed down for thousands of years. They occupied the area from southern Manitoba west to the Rocky Mountains and north to the North Saskatchewan River. Many Canadian Plains people had territories that went across today's boundary with the United States.

When the Europeans arrived, there were four groups of Plains people: Plains Cree, Stoney, Sarcee, and Blackfoot.

Where the People Lived

The dry, short grass of the prairie and foothills supported millions of bison. Many other animals lived there as well: moose, elk, mule deer, antelope, mountain sheep, and mountain goats. There were game birds and waterfowl. Roots and berry bushes also provided food.

The Plains people were **nomadic**, which means they followed the bison from place to place.

The Languages They Spoke

The Canadian Plains people speak three completely different languages. The Blackfoot Nation and Plains Cree speak the *Algonquian* language. The Stoney speak *Siouan*. The Sarcee speak *Athapaskan*. The three language families are as different from one another as English is from Chinese. To communicate with one another, the Plains people used sign language.

Shelter

Plains families lived in tipis. Tipis were cone-shaped tents sewn from animal skins and draped over a framework of poles. The poles were tied together at the top. Inside the tipi was a fireplace. The smoke from the fire escaped through an open hole at the top.

The Plains people sometimes decorated their tipis with designs and animal figures.

The Clothes the People Wore

People wore leather clothes made from animal **hides** of deer, elk, and moose. Clothes were sewn with **sinew** thread using a bone **awl** and needle. Men wore **leggings**, moccasins, and perhaps a shirt or robe of hide or fur. In winter they wore warmer moccasins and a hat and mitts.

Women wore shorter leggings with a dress and moccasins. They wore robes as outer clothing.

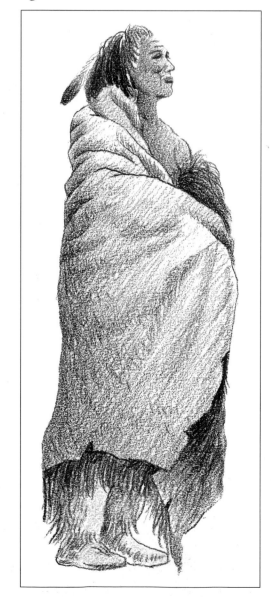

The buffalo robe kept the Plains people warm in winter.

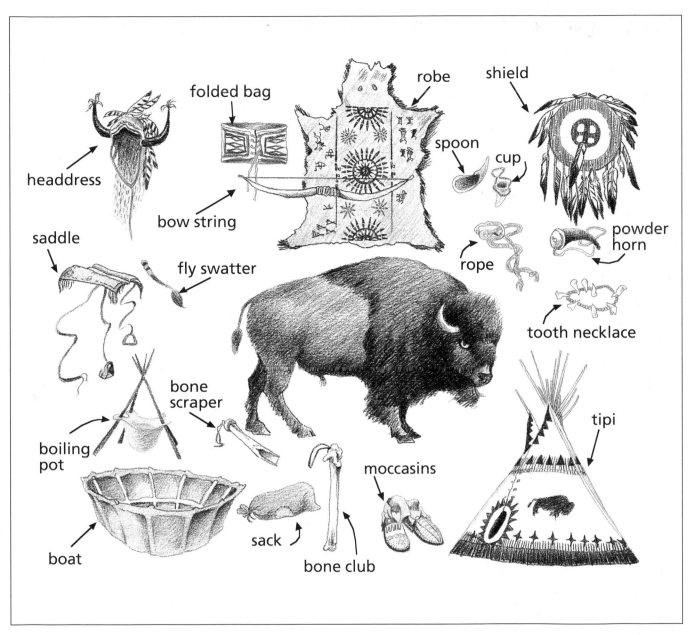

Bison were important to the Plains people. Parts of this animal could be used to make things.

 **READING PICTURES**

Look at the picture on this page showing the uses of bison.

1. Choose three objects in this picture.
2. Explain how you think the Plains people would have used these objects.

Transportation: How the People Moved About

Before horses arrived, the Plains people walked everywhere. They used dogs to carry packs and pull **travois**. The Plains Cree and Stoney used birch bark canoes to travel on rivers in the summer.

Europeans brought the horse to the Plains people. The horse completely changed Plains **society**. It could haul a much larger travois than a dog. It helped people travel much longer distances and hunt more easily than before.

How the People Were Organized

The Plains people were organized in **bands** made up of many families who were related to one another. The bands' leaders led by example and made decisions by discussion with others.

In the summer, the bands joined with other bands. Several thousand people hunted bison, held **religious ceremonies**, told stories, and visited. People played games, gambled, danced, sang, worked, and held meetings.

Men and women had different roles in Plains society, but each owned and controlled his and her own property.

Religion: What the People Believed

The Plains people believed that a power was present in every living thing. If a person could own this power, he or she could succeed in hunting or curing the sick. To find this power, young men and women went to a lonely spot to pray and **fast**.

In a few days a **vision** of a bear, a wolf, or a bison appeared to them in a dream to give them the power. This animal might give them a song to sing or a holy object, such as a feather or animal skin. The young person

The Plains people used the travois to move from place to place. Explain how the travois worked by studying this picture.

then kept this sacred object in a **medicine bundle**.

Crowfoot, the chief of the Blackfoot, spoke of a bison spirit that appeared to him. The vision told him to make a pair of leggings from a bison hide. These were his holy **charm.**

The bands met every summer. The people would then take part in a religious ceremony called a *Sun Dance*. The Sun Dance re-enacted stories about how certain powers had been given to the people.

The Plains Groups

THE BLACKFOOT NATION

Three tribes make up the Blackfoot Nation: the Blood, Blackfoot, and Peigan.

Blood

The Blood call themselves *Kainai*, which means "many chiefs" in their language. They speak the same language as the Blackfoot and Peigan. The language is called Algonquian. At the time the Europeans came, the Blood lived from the Red Deer River to the Belly River. In the mid-1800s, they moved farther south. They often moved south into Montana in the United States.

The Blood were buffalo hunters. They were also known as strong warriors. The population of the Blood in the 1800s was about 3000. In 1877 Chief Red Crow signed

Treaty Number 7 with the Canadian government. He remained leader of the tribe until his death in 1900.

In 1880 the Blood moved to a **reserve** between the St. Mary River and Belly River. It is the largest reserve in Canada today.

Blackfoot

The Blackfoot tribe is the smallest of the three tribes that make up the Blackfoot Nation. In their own language, they are called *Sksikaw*, which means "black foot" or "black feet." They speak the same language as the Blood and Peigan. At the time the Europeans came, the Blackfoot tribe lived along the Battle River and Red Deer River. Their population during that time was between 2000 and 3000.

These Blackfoot men are performing a tobacco ceremony in 1903. Describe what they are doing and what they are wearing.

The Blackfoot tribe were buffalo hunters and warriors. Crowfoot was the great leader of the Blackfoot tribe in the 1800s. In 1877 the Blackfoot tribe signed Treaty Number 7 and took a reserve at Blackfoot Crossing, east of Calgary. Today they number about 3500.

Peigan

The Peigan form the largest of the three tribes of the Blackfoot Nation. Their name comes from the Blackfoot word *Apiku'ni*, which means "badly tanned robe." They speak the same language as the Blood and Blackfoot. The Peigan once occupied a vast hunting ground along the foothills of the Rocky Mountains south into Montana. They travelled as far north as Fort Edmonton.

The Peigan signed Treaty Number 7 with the Canadian government. They selected a reserve near Pincher Creek. Today the population is about 2000.

SARCEE

The Sarcee are a **Dene** people who now live on a reserve outside Calgary. The Sarcee call themselves *Tsuut'ina*, meaning "many people." The Sarcee were late comers to the plains. They likely split from a northern tribe, and **adapted** the plains way of life. They are the only Dene to take up the way of life of the plains, but they have kept their Athapaskan language. Their annual Indian Days celebration is popular. The Sarcee now number about 800.

STONEY

The Stoney got their name from a word that described their way of boiling food. They boiled water by heating stones and dropping them into the water. Then they put food in the boiling water.

Outside Alberta, the Stoney are called

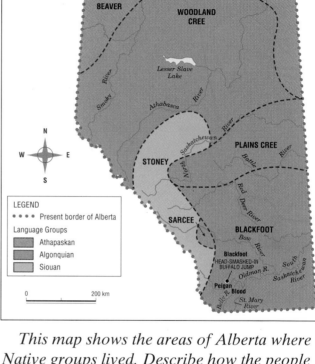

NATIVE TRIBES OF ALBERTA

This map shows the areas of Alberta where Native groups lived. Describe how the people moved across these areas to hunt, trade, or gather for celebrations.

Assiniboine. The Stoney are a Plains group who speak the Siouan language.

The Stoney once lived all across the plains. They were forced by their Blackfoot enemies to move north of the North Saskatchewan River. They were known for their fine *pemmican*. Pemmican is a food made by pounding dry meat into powder and mixing it with berries and fat. This food became very important to the European fur traders as well.

READING MAPS

Study the map showing Native Tribes of Alberta.

1. (a) Name the three languages spoken by the Native people of Alberta.
   (b) Which language group covered the largest area?
2. Choose two Native groups from the map. Read about those two groups in the text. Compare the lifestyles of the two groups.
3. Find out what Native group lives in an area of Alberta near you.

PLAINS CREE

The Plains Cree are very close relatives of the Woodland Cree. The Plains Cree came from Hudson Bay. They speak the Algonquian language. After they met the Europeans, some moved west to the plains. They stopped hunting and trapping in the forest. They became horse-mounted warriors and bison hunters. **Smallpox** killed many Plains Cree. The bison disappeared. The traditional way of life of the Plains Cree came to an end by the 1880s. They now live on reserves, where many ranch and farm.

The Woodland Natives

The Woodland Natives were the Chipewyan, Woodland Cree, Beaver, and Slavey.

Where the People Lived

The Woodland Cree lived in most of central Alberta. The Chipewyan lived to the east and the Beaver and Slavey to the west.

The Languages They Spoke

The Woodland Natives spoke two different languages. The Chipewyan, Slavey, and Beaver spoke Athapaskan. The Woodland Cree spoke Algonquian.

The Food the People Ate

The Woodland Natives thought of the land as their **storehouse.** The people hunted several large animals, including caribou, moose, mountain goats, and sheep. They knew where to move and when, according to the seasons. They hunted the animals with traps, bows and arrows, and spears. They fished using traps, nets, hooks and line, and spears. They also gathered berries and wild plants.

They roasted food over an open fire, or boiled it in a birch bark or hide container by adding hot rocks. They kept food from spoiling by drying and freezing it. They made a food called pemmican. All the Woodland Natives shared food with each other, no matter who had found it.

Transportation: How the People Moved About

In summer, the Woodland Natives travelled in light, birch bark canoes. They walked through the bush, carrying their belongings on their backs, supported by **tumplines** across their foreheads. In winter, they used snowshoes made of birch frames and **babiche** lacing. They hauled their belongings on toboggans.

A tumpline helped the Woodland Natives support heavy weights. Study this picture. Describe how the tumpline worked.

The Clothes the People Wore

The Woodland Natives made most clothing from leather. They tanned animal skins and sewed them into coats, shirts, dresses, leggings, trousers, moccasins, mitts, and hats. They often decorated their clothes with dyed moose hair, porcupine quills, shells, and **fringes.** They made warm robes from rabbit fur cut into strips and woven together.

Shelter

The Woodland Natives lived in tipis. Unlike the Plains people, however, they often covered their tipis with slabs of bark. A traveller might make a simple shelter by leaning two poles against a tree and covering it with hides and brush. Each tipi had a

fireplace. Fires were made with bow drills or by carrying coals to a new camp. A bow drill was a tool that made fire by rubbing a bow across a stick.

How the People Were Organized

The Woodland Natives were organized into small groups called local bands. Each band had between 25 and 50 people who were related to one another. Bands travelled in certain areas. If food was hard to find, they would move to another area.

At certain times of the year, bands came together for religious ceremonies and social activities. The people mostly made their own decisions.

Religion: What the People Believed

The Woodland Natives lived in close **harmony** with nature. A Woodland Cree warrior named Fineday said, "Everything has the spirit of **Manitou** in it, even a blade of grass, or else the grass could not grow."

This spirit made it possible for the people to live. They believed that they had to show respect for the animals they killed. If they did not, they believed the animals would not allow themselves to be hunted again. Then the people would have no more food.

Boys and girls often tried to find a spirit helper through dreams. The spirit would share its wisdom and help a person in everyday life. It would tell the person where to hunt or how to cure an illness.

One who found a spirit helper might become a **shaman**, with the power to tell the future and heal the sick.

The Woodland Natives told myths and legends that explain how the world was created. Myths taught people how to behave toward one another, nature, and the spirit world. They kept the **traditions** and history of the people.

When a person died, it was believed that the soul went to a spirit world. Drums were played to help the soul on its way.

Chipewyan

One group of Woodland Natives is the Chipewyan. They call themselves Dene or "people." The name Chipewyan was given to them by the Cree. It means "pointed skins," referring to the way they dried beaver skin. In the 1800s they lived across northern Manitoba, Saskatchewan, and Alberta.

The Chipewyan speak Athapaskan and are close relatives of the Slavey.

The Europeans entered Chipewyan land in 1717, when the Hudson's Bay Company built Fort Churchill on Hudson Bay. Many Chipewyan hunted beaver in the northern forests. Today, many Chipewyan have returned to a traditional way of life, based on hunting caribou. Today they number about 8400.

Woodland Cree

The Cree came originally from a group of Natives near James Bay. They use the name "Cree" only when speaking or writing in English, for they have other names for themselves. Cree live in a greater area than any other Native group in Canada, from Alberta to Quebec. In Alberta they call themselves *Nehiyawok*. Here, they form two groups: Plains Cree and Woodland Cree. Both speak the same Algonquian language.

The ancestors of the Cree have lived in the woodlands for at least 7000 years. They hunted moose, caribou, geese, ducks, and fish. They travelled by birch bark canoe in summer and by snowshoes and toboggan in winter. They lived in dome-shaped tipis. They wore leather clothes and made tools from wood, bone, hide, and stone.

Today, many Woodland Cree live in the city for much of the year. Their population when the Europeans came was about 30 000. Today they number about 122 000.

Joseph Dion was a **Metis** who visited the Woodland Cree. He wrote the following account.

IN THEIR OWN WORDS
Joseph Dion Tells About the Daily Life of the Woodland Cree

▼

"The life of the Woodland Cree was not easy. We had to be out in all kinds of weather, always hunting for something to eat.

We lived on the shores of the many large lakes that dot the forests. The Crees lived by these lakes long before the white man ever touched the shores.

If a Cree Indian wished to paint his face red or black, it was his own whim . . . The eagle feather hat represented bravery for it had to be earned the hard way. It could not just be made and worn by anybody.

The Woodland Crees made their moccasins from the hide of a deer or moose. Fur moccasins were often worn by women and children. These were usually made from bear skin but they were not so long lasting.

For relaxation the men often spent their time competing in sports of many kinds. Foot racing was always popular. The hoop game was a favorite. A hoop was rolled swiftly back and forth. The receiving side shot at it as it sped past and every miss meant the loss of an arrow. Among our rougher games, wrestling either on foot or on horseback was popular.

The first thing in the morning the elder of the home gave thanks to the Father of All for seeing another day. [When a young son had his first successful hunt], a number of guests would come to wish him a long and prosperous life. The little daughter was celebrated when she picked her first berry or brought in her first stick of wood or bit of water.

Once or twice a year the Cree would gather together for a celebration. In mid-summer they would hunt on the prairie. **"**

---

white man - *Europeans*
whim - *a fancy or notion*
elder - *an older person in a tribe whom others go to for wisdom and advice*
prosperous - *successful*

▲

Beaver

The Beaver live in the Peace River area of British Columbia and Alberta. They speak the Athapaskan language. They used to live in small nomadic bands, hunting bison, moose, caribou, and bears. The hunts were led by religious leaders called **dreamers**. Beaver children went into the bush on vision **quests** to gain power from the animals. The Beaver now live on reserves in British Columbia and Alberta.

Slavey

The Slavey live in the woodlands of northern Alberta. They are close relatives of the Beaver and Chipewyan. They are Dene, who speak Athapaskan.

The Slavey lived by fishing, hunting moose and caribou, and by gathering plants and berries. In winter the Slavey camped in groups or local bands of between 10 and 30 related people. In summer these groups came together briefly near the shores of a major lake for religious activities.

The Slavey first met Europeans when the explorer Alexander Mackenzie passed through in 1789. Soon after, fur trading posts were built on their lands. The Slavey in Alberta signed **Treaty Number 8** in 1899.

Conflict and Change

The Native people felt the effects of the Europeans long before they met them face to face. Other Native groups brought them European goods, such as tools.

The greatest change came from an animal the Europeans brought with them: the horse. Spanish explorers brought the horse to Mexico first. In time, horses made their way north to the plains. The Blackfoot did not have a name for this creature when they first saw it. They called it "big dog" because it served humans like a dog would.

With horses the people could carry more, including extra food for hard times. It was easier to hunt the bison, to travel, and to fight their enemies. By the 1730s the Plains people had horses. Some Woodland Natives also had horses, but at a later time.

Fur Trade Days

For more than 100 years, Europeans and Native people met together to trade. Native life went on much as before, although the trade goods changed everyday life. The Native people soon replaced their stone tools and arrowheads with metal. They began to use cloth made in Europe for their clothing.

The fur traders, however, also carried deadly diseases. Many thousands of Native people died from these diseases. The Europeans also brought alcohol, which spread disease and destruction among the Native people. Meanwhile, the bison herds, which once numbered in the tens of millions, were slaughtered by the newcomers. The lifestyle of the Natives was threatened by disease, alcohol, and starvation.

Treaties and Reserves

In 1870 the new country of Canada took control of the vast *Northwest*. The Northwest included the plains and woodlands that you have been reading about. Many Canadians believed that the plains would someday be covered in farms. They knew that Native people had certain **rights** to the land. They made agreements with them, called **treaties**.

In exchange for their land, the treaties offered Native people smaller pieces of land, called reserves. Some treaties also promised to give the Native people tools, farm animals, hunting and fishing rights, money, and clothes.

The Native people had little choice except to sign treaties with Canada. If they did not sign, they might have to fight a war they might not win. They also signed treaties because most of the great bison herds had disappeared by the 1870s. Many Plains people faced starvation. The treaties offered them ways to feed themselves.

A few Native groups refused at first to sign treaties. For example, Cree families following Big Bear did not want to live on a little reserve. In later years, however, starvation forced most of them to sign. In 1882 even Big Bear accepted treaty payments so that his few remaining followers could survive the winter.

THE NORTHWEST

Northwest is a word used to describe the huge area north and west of Lake Superior. It is sometimes spelled North-West. Fur traders and explorers used this name to describe what we now call Manitoba, Saskatchewan, Alberta, the Yukon, and the Northwest Territories. Today, Northwest refers to the area north of Alberta.

Crowfoot was known to his people as someone who could face danger and survive. He became one of the three head chiefs of the Blackfoot in 1870.

CROWFOOT

Crowfoot was a chief of the Blackfoot tribe. He was born to the Blood people near Belly River around the year 1830. As a teenager, he showed great bravery. Among the Blood, the greatest glory did not go to someone who killed the enemy. Glory went to someone who could face danger and survive. During one battle, Crowfoot rode on horse into the camp of the enemy Crow people. There he touched one of the Crow tipis with his spear, turned around, and rode away. This is how he got his name "Crow Indian's Big Foot," which was shortened to Crowfoot.

Crowfoot was a wise leader. In 1870 he became one of the three head chiefs of the Blackfoot tribe. He kept good relations with the fur traders. He made peace with the Cree. In 1874 he welcomed the North-West Mounted Police.

The Blackfoot tribe settled on their reserve in 1881. Crowfoot became unhappy with the Canadians because they treated his people badly. Nevertheless, when the Metis and some Native groups took up arms against the Canadians, he refused to let his people join. He was angry with the Canadians, but he did not want to lead his people into a fight that they could not win.

RED CROW

Red Crow was a head chief of the Blood tribe. He was an important leader who helped settle the West peacefully.

Red Crow became chief in 1870. Four years later, he greeted the North-West Mounted Police as friends in 1874. Because he trusted them, he signed Treaty 7 three years later. The treaty placed his people on a reserve. He helped his people on the reserve by introducing ranching, and he stressed the importance of education. He also encouraged them to keep Native **customs** and religion.

This picture shows Crowfoot (the second person in the middle row) and Red Crow (sitting on Crowfoot's left) in 1886. Both men led their people during the time of the fur trade.

UNDERSTANDING THE PEOPLE

Read the stories about Crowfoot and Red Crow.

1. Compare how Crowfoot and Red Crow reacted to the changes brought by Europeans. Write a paragraph describing how their reactions were the same and how they were different.

 GATHERING INFORMATION

1. Where do archaeologists think the first peoples of North America come from?

2. Explain what is meant by the statement, "the Plains people were nomadic."

3. Compare the land where the Plains and the Woodland people lived.
   (a) How did the land affect what the Plains and Woodland people ate?
   (b) How did the land affect how these peoples moved about?

4. Think about the changes Europeans brought to Native life. Did European ideas and goods improve the way Natives lived? Give reasons for your answer.

 **FURTHER STUDY**

You learned in this chapter that some Native groups refused to sign treaties at first. Today, the Lubicon are an example of a group that still has not signed a treaty.

1. Find out who the Lubicon are. Report your findings to the class.

1754 Anthony Henday spends the winter near Edmonton

1788 The North West Company founds Fort Chipewyan

1821 The North West Company and the Hudson's Bay Company unite

1874 The North-West Mounted Police set out for Alberta

1778 Peter Pond is the first European to reach Athabasca River

1792 Alexander Mackenzie travels up the Peace River, and reaches the Pacific Ocean

1873 Cypress Hills Massacre

CHAPTER FOCUS

In the 1700s, Europeans came to Alberta to find new fur trade routes. Soon, the fur trade grew in the West.

How did the Native people help the explorers and fur traders who came to Alberta?

How did the fur traders live? How did they get to Alberta?

What did fur traders give Native people in exchange for furs? How did Natives and European fur traders influence each other's lifestyles?

Who were the first Europeans to come to Alberta?

CHAPTER 2

THE FUR TRADE:
The Coming of the Europeans

The Bay Men Come West

In 1754, Anthony Henday travelled where no European had gone before. He worked for the **Hudson's Bay Company.** He and his Cree **guides** started their journey from Hudson Bay in June. They paddled across the prairie along the Saskatchewan River. Then they walked. They met many different groups of Native people. By autumn they were near the present-day city of Red Deer. Here they met the Blackfoot, who ruled the southern plains.

Anthony Henday: First European in the West

Anthony Henday spent the winter with the Blackfoot near present-day Edmonton. He was the first European to visit what we now call Alberta. He wanted to meet the people and to ask them to bring their furs to the fur trading posts on Hudson Bay. There, the Natives could trade their furs for European goods.

Not long after Henday's trip, another traveller arrived in Alberta. His name was Peter Pond. He was a fur trader from

The great popularity of the beaver hat in Europe gave rise to the fur trade in Canada. The beaver fur was pounded into felt, which made the finest hats.

Montreal. In 1778, he became the first white man to reach the Athabasca River. He spent the winter there. Here he met many Cree and Chipewyan who usually had to go to Hudson Bay to trade their furs. They were very happy to see Pond because he brought his trading goods with him. By selling their furs to him, they would not have to make the long and dangerous journey to Hudson Bay.

A New Company: the Nor' Westers

Pond had been gone so long that his partners thought he was dead. When Pond got back the next summer with thousands of valuable beaver furs, they were amazed. Encouraged by his success, Pond and several other traders formed a new company, called the North West Company. The people who worked for them were called "Nor' Westers." The North West Company began to build fur trade posts along rivers in present-day Alberta.

The beaver is found in forest areas all around Canada. In the library, research the habits of the beaver. Why was its fur so valuable?

Pond was a hot-tempered man. He was accused of murdering two fur traders. The company Pond started made a lot of money, but he died in poverty.

Pond drew maps of his travels. On one map, he showed a large river flowing northward to the Arctic Ocean. On another, he showed a river flowing westward to the Pacific Ocean. Explorers had tried to find a way to the Pacific for a long time. Inspired by Pond's ideas, Alexander Mackenzie took up the challenge.

The Travels of Alexander Mackenzie

Alexander Mackenzie worked for the North West Company. He made two of the greatest voyages of exploration in Canadian history. He entered the fur trade when he was only 15 years old. In 1788 he had a fort built at Lake Athabasca. He called it Fort Chipewyan because the Chipewyan lived in the area. This fort was the first European settlement in present-day Alberta.

Alexander Mackenzie was an explorer who travelled across western Canada. What was he looking for?

In 1789 Mackenzie used Fort Chipewyan as a starting point for his first great voyage of exploration. He wanted to find Pond's route to the Pacific Ocean. The river that he followed, however, took him north instead of west. After paddling thousands of kilometres down the longest river in Canada, he ended up at the Arctic Ocean, just as the Natives told him he would. That great river now bears his name, the Mackenzie River. It is also known as the Dehcho ("great") River.

In 1793, Mackenzie tried again. This time he travelled up the Peace River, crossed the Rocky Mountains, and reached the Pacific Ocean. He was the first European to travel all the way across North America. On a point of land overlooking the Pacific Ocean, Mackenzie mixed some red dye and grease together and wrote on a rock:

> *Alexander Mackenzie, from Canada, by land, the twenty-second of July, one thousand seven hundred and ninety-three.*

That rock is still there. The words faded over time, but have been replaced so we can read them today.

Mackenzie's voyages proved that the fur traders could travel by river all the way from Montreal to the Pacific Ocean. Many of the important points along that route lay in present-day Alberta. It was the fur trade that first tied Alberta to Canada.

Mackenzie's great voyages would not have been possible without the birch bark canoe. It had been used by Native people for hundreds of years.

The fur traders learned to use canoes from the Native people.

Fur Trade Rivalry

Mackenzie reported that the Natives were glad to see the fur traders come to their territory. The Hudson's Bay Company feared that it would lose all its trade to the North West Company. It sent its own explorers, Peter Fidler and David Thompson, to the Alberta region. They explored and mapped the Athabasca and Saskatchewan rivers in the 1790s and early 1800s. In 1797 Thompson left the Hudson's Bay Company and joined the North West Company.

The Hudson's Bay Company and the North West Company built fur trade forts along rivers into present-day Alberta. Wherever one company built a fur trade post, the other built one nearby. These posts were the beginnings of several communities of present-day Alberta.

In his *Journals* Mackenzie wrote a description of the fur trade at Fort Chipewyan. It had been his headquarters for eight years.

IN THEIR OWN WORDS

Mackenzie Describes the Fur Trade

▼

"The canoes which leave Lake la Pluie about the first of August, do not arrive here till the end of September . . . when [some of them are] sent up to the Peace River . . . to the Slave River and Lake, or beyond . . . the rest of the people remain here to trade with the Chipewyans.

In the fall of the year the natives meet the traders at the forts, where they [trade] furs. [They] do not return till the beginning of the year.

Till the year 1782, the people of Athabasca sent or carried their furs regularly to Fort Churchill, at Hudson's Bay . . . The difference of the price set on goods here and [there] made it [necessary for] the Chipewyans, to undertake a journey of five or six months, in the course of which they often lost their lives from hunger. "

▲

 **UNDERSTANDING THE STORY**

Read Alexander Mackenzie's description of the fur trade.

1. How long did it take the canoes to get from Lake la Pluie to the Slave River?
2. Why did the Chipewyan travel for five or six months to Fort Churchill?
3. Make up an interview with a Chipewyan trader. Ask him about the dangers of undertaking such a long journey.

End of the Fur Trade Rivalry

The fur trade was the main occupation of the Europeans from Mackenzie's time until the 1880s. **Competition** between the Hudson's Bay Company and the North West Company finally forced them to join in 1821. The new Hudson's Bay Company ruled the fur trade and the Western region for another 50 years.

Fur traders carried the furs and trade goods on their backs. They also paddled the birch bark canoe.

Fur trade posts were built along the river routes. Fort Edmonton was one of the most important fur trade posts.

Life at the Fur Trade Posts

Fort Edmonton was the centre of the fur trade in Alberta. The fur traders brought blankets, metal tools such as axes, and other goods to Fort Edmonton from Hudson Bay. They used these goods to trade with the Native people for furs. Fort Edmonton was a convenient place to stop. Here the traders could rest awhile. From here they could head north to Athabasca country or west to Rocky Mountain House.

This photograph shows Fort Edmonton in 1871. Fort Edmonton was built on a cliff above the North Saskatchewan River.

The arrival of the fur traders at Fort Edmonton was cause for celebration. The first boats were greeted with booming cannons as they rounded the river bend and came in sight of the fort.

There were few children at the fort. They would have been very excited to see the boats appear on the river. They would plug their ears when the cannons roared and would run to the river's edge to see the first boat arrive.

In fur trade days, Fort Edmonton stood on a steep hill overlooking the North Saskatchewan River. It had high wooded walls for protection. Most of the people living there were men. They packed and unpacked the boats. They built and repaired most of the boats used in the fur trade. The men built about 12 new boats each year. These boats could not be used on the fast-moving rivers in other parts of Canada. But they were easy to row on the slow-moving streams in the prairies.

At the fort, the traders would celebrate, relax, and then move on. The people who lived at the fort ate buffalo meat, which they bought from the Metis. They grew some potatoes. They also ground wheat into flour at the windmill, which stood on a hill behind the fort.

James Hector's First Trip to Rocky Mountain House

From Fort Edmonton, the fur traders would set out for Rocky Mountain House, another fur trade fort. In 1858, young James Hector made his first trip to Rocky Mountain House. He was in charge of several boats and he was very nervous. The men rowed the boats up the North Saskatchewan River towards the mountains. The river was long but quiet. It was on the edge of Blackfoot country. Hector and his men were going to trade with the Blackfoot.

As the boats came near the fort, the men in the first canoe spotted the Blackfoot camp. The Blackfoot got up from around the fire and watched the boats go by. The Blackfoot had travelled a long way from the south to meet the fur traders.

Many ceremonies took place before the trading began. The Blackfoot considered trading to be more than just an exchange of goods. Trading was also a sign of friendship. This friendship needed to be renewed with speeches and gifts.

A day was set for trading. On that day, Hector went out from the fort to meet the Blackfoot chief. The chief told Hector that he hoped that the traders would treat his people fairly. The chief showed he was a generous man. He piled buffalo robes and dried buffalo meat on the back of a horse and gave it to Hector. Hector gave the chief blankets and cloth in return.

Although the traders and Blackfoot said they were friends, the traders kept the fort gates closed. The traders invited a few Blackfoot at a time into a special trading room. The trade began. Each side argued for better deals. Since no money was used, the two sides had to agree on how many furs or buffalo robes it took to buy a blanket, or a gun, or a kettle.

This time the trading went peacefully. The other traders, however, told Hector that this was not always so. Sometimes the traders would run out of trade goods. Then a pile of robes would be traded for a little parcel of sugar or tea. The Blackfoot would feel cheated and arguments would follow. Sometimes shots would be fired in anger and people would be killed.

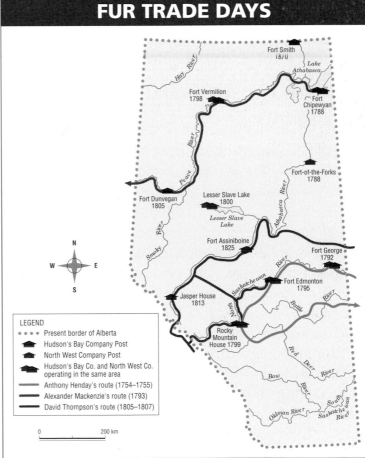

The first Europeans came to Alberta to trade with the Native people for furs. Why did the Europeans build their fur trading posts on rivers?

READING MAPS

Study the map called "Fur Trade Days" on page 23.

1. Pick one of the three explorers' routes shown on the map. Why did this explorer come to Alberta? What river route did he follow?

2. Find as many fur trade posts as you can on the map. Explain why they are located where they are.

3. What kinds of transportation did the fur traders use? Where did they learn this kind of transportation?

From Co-operation to Conflict

For many years, the fur traders and the Native people lived peacefully together in the West. They **co-operated** in the fur trade. The traders needed the Native people to trap the furs, to supply them with food, and to act as guides and translators. In turn, the Native people grew to depend on the metal tools, cloth, guns, and other trade goods the Europeans brought.

This situation began to change by the 1870s. Furs became harder to find. Although the North West Company disappeared in 1821, a new group of traders appeared on the plains.

The Wolfers

Some American traders called wolfers began coming into Canada. They were called wolfers because they left poisoned buffalo meat on the prairie to kill the wolves. The Natives did not like the wolfers because the poison also killed many of their valuable dogs.

In 1873 a group of wolfers was sleeping near Fort Benton, in Montana. Next morning they discovered that some of their horses were missing. They thought that Natives must have stolen them. The Americans considered stealing horses a very serious crime.

The angry wolfers headed north into Canada to get their horses back. They met a group of Assiniboine Natives in the Cypress Hills of southern Saskatchewan. One of the wolfers claimed that these Natives had stolen his horse. The wolfers rode into the Assiniboine camp.

The Cypress Hills Massacre

Nobody is sure what happened next. Apparently, the Assiniboine grew angry that the wolfers had marched into their camp and called them thieves. The wolfers then jumped into a ditch and began to fire their guns wildly at the Natives, killing many of them. The young Natives tried to charge the ditch but they were killed one by one.

That night, the wolfers came into the Native camp again. They killed the chief, called Little Soldier, and many women and children. When the killing stopped, at least 20 Natives and one wolfer lay dead.

Newspapers in Montana called these white men heroes. They said the wolfers had won a battle. In Canada, people called the incident a massacre. A massacre is the killing of innocent people. This event came to be known as the Cypress Hills Massacre.

Many Canadians felt something had to be done to stop the wolfers and other Americans from coming across the border.

Fort Whoop-Up

For years Canadians had complained about the American traders who crossed the border and carried off hundreds of thousands of furs and buffalo robes. The American traders fought the Natives and fought one another. They sold a deadly drink to the Natives. It was a mixture of alcohol, tobacco, red ink, and other dangerous liquids. Violence spread throughout the territory and led to many deaths. The American traders even built their own forts on Canadian land. The most famous of their forts was Fort Whoop-Up. It was near present-day Lethbridge. They even flew the American flag over their posts.

Around the time of the Cypress Hills Massacre, Reverend John McDougall wrote that near Edmonton, "forty-two able bodied men . . . were slain . . . There was no law . . . whole camps went on the spree . . . shooting, stabbing, killing, freezing, dying." The fur trade, which had begun in co-operation and brought benefit to both Natives and whites, was now bringing disaster to the plains.

Fort Whoop-Up was an American fort built on Canadian land.

In Ottawa, Prime Minister Sir John A. Macdonald feared that the coming of the American traders might cause Canada to lose control of the West. He organized a new police force, called the North-West Mounted Police, to go to "Whoop-Up country," where Fort Whoop-Up was.

Life on the open plains attracted adventurous young men to the new force. The first 150 joined in the fall of 1873 and spent the winter in Manitoba. They were joined the next summer by another 150 men.

The Great March West

On July 8, 1874, the 300 Mounties (North-West Mounted Police officers) set out from Dufferin, Manitoba for Whoop-Up country, some 1300 kilometres away. They were led by Colonel George French. He organized the force like an army. Each day they rose at dawn and rode their horses in a long, slow column. Almost 200 carts, pulled by oxen, followed with their supplies.

The grass was dry that summer and many of the horses died. Some of the men died too, and some gave up and ran away. The men arrived hungry and thirsty in early September near the Bow and Belly Rivers. They hoped to find Fort Whoop-Up. But the men were lost. Colonel French travelled south to Montana where he hired a guide, named Jerry Potts.

Jerry Potts's Native name was Ky-yo-kosi, meaning "Bear Child." His mother was a Blood Native and his father was a Scot. He was famous among the Blackfoot Nation as a great warrior and hunter. He helped the Mounties. Potts taught the Blackfoot Nation and the Mounties about each other. He also made sure they got along together. He led the

Jerry Potts helped the Blackfoot Nation and the Mounties to get along with each other.

police to Fort Whoop-Up. Most of the Americans fled before the Mounties arrived.

Potts then took the Mounties to an island in the Oldman River. They built Fort Macleod there. The fort was named for James Macleod, who was French's assistant. Macleod wanted to have good relations with the Natives. He demanded high standards of behaviour from his men.

The following summer the Mounties built Fort Calgary on the Bow River and Fort Walsh in the Cypress Hills. These forts were patrol posts for the Mounties. In 1876 another major patrol post was set up at Battleford. Each year more patrol posts were built until they were in all parts of the Northwest.

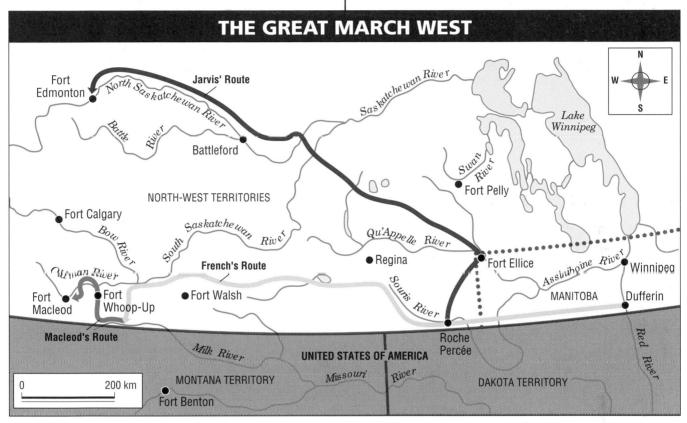

THE GREAT MARCH WEST

This map shows the route taken by the North-West Mounted Police in 1874. The march began in Dufferin, Manitoba. The Mounties split into two groups at Roche Percée. George French led the larger group on a southern route towards Fort Whoop-Up. William Jarvis led the smaller group on a northern route to Fort Edmonton.

 **READING MAPS**

Study the map called "The Great March West."

1. Follow the route from Dufferin and along the yellow line to Roche Percée. Choose the southern route and follow it west. Where did the Mounties following this route stop?

   (Note: Alberta belonged to an area called the North-west Territories at the time of the Great March West.)

2. Find Fort Whoop-Up on the map. Explain why the Mounties came to Fort Whoop-Up.

3. Read the text and describe some of the experiences of the Mounties. Explain the role the Mounties had in settling Alberta.

Rise of the Metis Nation

Origin of the Name Metis

Metis is one of several words used to describe people of mixed Native and European **origin**. The word *métis* is an old French word meaning "mixed."

The Metis in western Canada were the children of the fur traders and their Native wives. Most were French and **Catholic,** though some had English-speaking **Protestant** fathers. The Metis soon formed their own **culture,** combining the lifestyles of Europeans and Natives.

Metis Daily Life

Music played an important part in the daily life of the Metis. Every fiddler knew the music for jigs and reels. These were lively dances borrowed from the Scots and the French. The music lasted long into the night, until the dancers' moccasins wore out.

The Metis style of clothing came from both Natives and Europeans. They wore colourful sashes with belts around their waists. Early clothes were made of animal skins and decorated with beads. The Metis were admired for the beautiful flower designs on their clothing. Natives called them the "flower beadwork people."

Explain why Native people called the Metis the "flower beadwork people." What was the origin of the word "Metis"?

READING PICTURES

Study the picture of the three Metis on page 28.

1. Describe the clothing of each person in this picture.

2. Explain how the Metis style of clothing shows both European and Native influence. Point out specific things that look Native or European.

3. In what other ways did the Metis combine a European and a Native lifestyle?

The Bison Hunt

The Metis learned the bison hunt from the Plains people. Every year, hunters and their families travelled together on the prairie with their horses and carts. They prepared for the hunt by **electing** a captain of the hunt. The captain would be someone brave, good at shooting, and a fine horseman.

After the hunt, the women cut up the animals and loaded the meat onto carts. Later they dried the meat and used it to make pemmican, which they sold to the fur traders.

Every year Metis hunters and their families went on the bison hunt. Explain how the Metis lifestyle was a mix of both the Native people and the European.

Changing Times

The Metis were in the very centre of the fur trade. They worked as interpreters, supplied food, and trapped. They also moved furs and supplies across the plains in their Red River carts.

The Metis, however, resented the many Canadian settlers who came from Ontario and settled on their land.

To protect their **rights,** the Metis rebelled against the Canadians in 1869 and in 1885. The Canadians sent soldiers to put down the rebellions. Many people died. The Metis leader, Louis Riel, was hanged for **treason**.

The Move to Alberta

The Metis were given farm land around Red River in Manitoba after the rebellions. They found the change from hunting bison to farming difficult. Most Metis sold their land and many moved west to Catholic **missions** around Fort Edmonton. These missions included St. Albert, Lac St. Anne, and Lac la Biche.

Many Metis lived in **poverty** after the rebellions. When the bison disappeared and the fur trade died out, some Metis worked in railway and logging camps. Some also hunted, trapped, and fished.

The Metis Settlements

During the 1920s and 1930s, the Metis fought to be able to own their land. In 1932 they formed the Metis **Association** of Alberta. This association was the first Metis **organization** in Canada.

The Alberta government finally set up a series of farms across northern Alberta. Today, these Metis Settlements are managed by Metis themselves. Metis make their living

JAMES MCKAY

James McKay was born at Fort Edmonton in 1828. His father was a Scottish guide and his mother was Metis. He guided Red River carts. These carts moved fur and supplies to fur trade posts throughout the West. He later started a business running a stagecoach from Winnipeg to Edmonton.

McKay spoke English, French, Ojibwa, Cree, and Sioux. He helped Canadians and Natives make treaties because he could understand these languages. Later he became a powerful politician in the new province of Manitoba. He always dressed in his Metis clothes.

James McKay was a Metis. How did he keep his Metis lifestyle after he became a politician?

by farming, fishing, ranching, and logging. The Metis are now recognized in Canada's **Constitution** with the Native peoples.

Europeans in the West

Europeans came to the West because they wanted to trade with Native people. The Europeans traded goods for furs. The Hudson's Bay Company and the North West Company built fur trading posts along rivers in the West.

Native people and Metis were important to the fur trade. The Native people traded with the Europeans. Metis acted as interpreters for the Europeans and Native people. Metis also helped the Europeans move furs across the West.

The North-West Mounted Police came to the West after the Cypress Hills Massacre. They set up patrol posts to keep law and order in the West.

Although there were European fur traders and Mounties, there were not many European people living in the West. The government of Canada, however, would soon begin a campaign to settle large numbers of Europeans in the West.

GATHERING INFORMATION

1. Who was the first European to visit the Northwest?
2. What were the names of the two fur trading companies that explored and built forts in the Northwest?
3. What trade goods did the fur traders have that the Native people wanted? What did the Native people give in exchange for these goods?
4. You are a Native person going to the fur trade post. Make a shopping list of goods you want.
5. Why did Canada send the North-West Mounted Police to Whoop-Up country?
6. What does the word Metis mean?
   (a) How were the Metis involved in the fur trade?
   (b) Explain how the Metis created a new lifestyle.

FURTHER STUDY

1. Make your own map of Alberta. On your map,
   (a) label the rivers explored and named by the North West Company and Hudson's Bay Company.
   (b) create a legend and show where the North West Company and Hudson's Bay Company forts were located.
2. Pretend you are Alexander Mackenzie or James Hector. Describe what it was like to be an explorer or fur trader. Use your own words.
3. As a Native person, describe how the fur trade changed your way of life. You might want to discuss changes to hunting and the new goods introduced.
4. Look in the encyclopedia and read about Louis Riel. Write a paragraph about him.

1885 *The Canadian Pacific Railway (CPR) is completed*

1872 *Canadian government offers to sell land in the West to settlers*

1901 *The population of Alberta reaches 73 000*

1867 *Canada becomes a country*

1870 *Canada purchases the Northwest*

1876 *The first ranchers arrive in Alberta*

1896 *Clifford Sifton begins a campaign to settle the West*

1906 *The population of Alberta reaches 185 000*

CHAPTER FOCUS

In the 1870s, the government of Canada bought the western lands that included what is now Alberta. The government wanted people to settle on these lands.

How did the government encourage settlers to come to Alberta?

Why did the Canadian government want people to settle in Alberta?

Why would people leave their homes and friends and move to a new land?

How did the newcomers help one another?

CHAPTER 3

RANCH AND FARM:
The Prairies Changed Forever

The West Becomes Part of Canada

Canada became a country in 1867. There were only four **provinces** at first: Ontario, Quebec, Nova Scotia, and New Brunswick. The great western lands still belonged to the Hudson's Bay Company.

Sir John A. Macdonald was the first prime minister of Canada. He knew that Canada needed more good farmland if it was to grow and do well. All of the best farmland in the four provinces had already been taken by farmers. Many people were moving from Canada to the United States in search of good land. Macdonald wanted these people to stay in Canada. He decided that Canada should buy the western lands from the Hudson's Bay Company. Canadians would then be able to settle on these lands.

No one knew if there was good farmland in the West. The Hudson's Bay Company, which did not want farmers in its territory, had always said the land was bad for farming. A British explorer named John Palliser agreed. He said that a large area of the West did not

*The **surveyors** measured the land so it could be divided up into farms.*

get enough rain to have good farmland. This dry part of the prairies came to be called the **Palliser Triangle**.

A Canadian explorer named Henry Youle Hind agreed with Palliser about the dryness of the West. However, he said that there was much fine farmland there. Sir John A. Macdonald believed him. Canada bought the western lands from the Hudson's Bay Company on July 15, 1870.

The government began preparing to settle people in the West. It signed treaties with Natives. It organized the North-West Mounted Police and sent them to enforce law in the West. Surveyors began to measure land. They divided it into millions of equal squares called **sections.**

Some land was given to railways to sell to farmers. The money from the sales went toward building the railways. Work began on a railway in southern Manitoba in 1875. But progress was slow.

The Canadian Pacific Railway was not finished until 1885. This railway went across the prairies. It allowed settlers to reach the western farmlands more easily than before.

In 1872 the Canadian government began to sell land to people who wanted to settle in the West. Anyone could buy one quarter of a section for $10. In return, settlers promised to build a house on the land. They also promised to plow a certain area each year. At the end of three years the settlers would get the **title** to their land. These quarter sections were called **homesteads.** The farmers who settled on them were called homesteaders.

The government hoped that people would come from all over the world to buy the cheap land in the West.

Round-Up Days: Ranching in Alberta

Ranchers first brought cattle into Alberta in the 1870s. The foothill country of southwestern Alberta is one of the best areas in North America for raising cattle. It has open grassland and sheltered valleys. In winter, the **chinooks** melt the snow and keep the hills bare. Cattle can **graze** on the grassland all year long.

Ranchers brought the first small herds to Alberta from Montana. Many members of the North-West Mounted Police became ranchers when they retired from the force. They were joined by wealthy Englishmen who thought ranching was an exciting life.

There was more interest in ranching when the railway reached the prairies in the 1880s. The ranchers could easily ship their beef to markets in Chicago or Toronto. From there the beef could be shipped all the way to Europe.

The railway, however, also brought settlers. Ranchers did not want them to come. Settlers put up fences and filled the open prairie with wheat fields. This meant cattle had less grassland to graze. However, the ranchers could not stop the settlers. The ranchers did not own the land. They merely rented it from the government. For a few years the ranchers were able to hold on to their best land for grazing. After 1905, however, the Canadian government began to sell off the best lands to settlers.

RODEO

Rodeo means **round-up**, or the gathering of cattle to be counted, inspected, and **branded**. Mexican cowboys were likely the first to show their skills as a sport. They used their *la reata* (rope) to catch and tie cattle.

The first Canadian rodeo show was held in Raymond, Alberta, in 1903. A few years later, Guy Weadick brought his "Wild West Show" from the United States to Canada. He and a group of businessmen organized the first Calgary Stampede in 1912. It lasted six days and attracted almost 100 000 people to watch.

Today rodeos are held at several places in Alberta. Rodeos bring back the days when cowboys made their living. Calf roping is one rodeo event that is still practised on ranches.

The rodeo arrived in Alberta in the 1880s. This photograph shows an event in the third Calgary Stampede in 1923. What real life skills are the rodeo events based on?

More and more settlers came. The ranchers then had a bad winter in 1906-1907. The chinook did not come. The snow covered the grass. The cattle could not eat the grass and many died.

Huge herds of cattle could no longer roam freely in Alberta, but ranching survived. Much of the land in southern Alberta was too dry for farming. As the settlers abandoned this land it was taken up again by the ranchers.

The Early Days of Ranching

Cowboys lived a **romantic** life in the early days of ranching, in the 1880s. Cattle raised themselves on the open prairie. The cowboys rounded up the cattle in the spring for branding and in the fall to ship them to market.

Cowboys spent most of the day on the backs of horses. They kept watch over the herds.

THE MOSQUITO CREEK ROUND-UP

F.W. Ing took part in the Mosquito Creek round-up of 1884. He set out with the Bar U wagons. There were about 20 men and at least 100 horses.

Like every cowboy, he had a slicker, which was a waterproof cape to keep him dry when it rained. He slept in a tent or under a blanket.

The men set out onto the wild prairie, east of where the city of Lethbridge now stands. They rounded up the cattle that had been set free to graze on the prairie grass. It took only a week to find most of the cattle, but it took two months to bring them back.

Each day Ing and the other cowboys rode out in circles. Each had to cover a different area. Ing brought his cattle back to camp where they became part of a growing herd.

Each day the herd grew larger. The men had to guard it day and night. As the round-up moved west towards Claresholm, the men separated the cattle marked with their brand. The cowboys then led their cattle to their own land.

Ranchers rounded up cattle to ship to markets in the fall. Why is Alberta good land for raising cattle?

JOHN WARE

John Ware was born a **slave** in the United States. After he was freed he drifted west to Texas where he found work on a ranch.

In the 1870s, he drove herds of Texas cattle north to Montana. In 1882 he helped bring 3000 cattle to the foothills near Calgary.

Ware learned that experienced cowboys were needed in Alberta. He decided to work for several large cattle companies there. Then he started his own ranch in the foothills in 1890. In 1900, he moved to a new ranch along the Red Deer River, east of Brooks.

John Ware was a successful rancher in Alberta in the 1890s.

MATTHEW HENRY COCHRANE

Matthew Henry Cochrane was a cattle rancher. He was born in Quebec in 1823. He had his start in the shoe business in Montreal.

Cochrane's real interest in life was ranching. Cochrane owned one of the largest ranches in Alberta. He **leased** a huge area west of Calgary. Today the town of Cochrane is named after him. You can visit his ranch in Cochrane today.

Matthew Henry Cochrane gave his name to a town in Alberta.

Homesteading on the Prairie

Except for Native people, Canada is a land of newcomers. For more than 300 years, people have come to Canada to build a better life.

Today most newcomers move to the cities of Canada. In earlier times, however, people came to settle on the land. The new settlers in eastern Canada had to clear the forest, build homes, find their own food and clothing, and survive the cold Canadian winter.

This story was repeated in Atlantic Canada, then Quebec, then Ontario. Now Canada hoped that the story would be repeated in the West.

A Disappointing Response

The Canadian government began to sell land in the West almost for free in 1872. There were not many European settlers there at that time. Soon the steel rails of the Canadian Pacific Railway crossed the prairie and went into the Rocky Mountains. Still, few people came to the West.

There were only about 1000 settlers in Alberta when the Canadian Pacific Railway reached Calgary in 1883. The railway wanted more settlers to come so that it could make money. It would make money by transporting the wheat that the settlers would grow. The wheat would be transported to markets in Ontario and Quebec.

The owners of the railway hoped to attract settlers by advertising the western lands. The owners printed millions of posters and **pamphlets** and sent them to the United States, Britain, and Western Europe. The owners also sent **agents** to speak at town halls and county fairs in those places. There was some response, but not much. In 1895, the railway had been in Alberta for ten years. But there were still only 26 000 settlers in Alberta.

The "Last Best West"

In 1896 Canada elected Wilfrid Laurier to be the new prime minister. "The twentieth century belongs to Canada," Laurier said. He believed that all Canada needed to become a great country was more people. Laurier chose Clifford Sifton to take charge of settling the West.

Sifton set to work immediately. First, he made it easier for settlers already in the West to find their land and get title to it. Next, he greatly increased the advertising of western lands. He used methods similar to the ones used by the Canadian Pacific Railway. Much of the advertising was sent to farmers in the United States, Britain, and Western Europe. The advertising declared, "Canada is the Last Best West!"

Perhaps Sifton's greatest success came from his decision to spend more time asking the poor farmers of Central and Eastern Europe to come to Canada. Sifton's agents seemed to be everywhere, spreading the word about the fine, cheap farmland in Canada.

This time, people came. By 1901, there were 73 000 people in Alberta. By 1906, there were 185 000.

This poster was made to make people from around the world want to settle in the Canadian prairies.

 **READING PICTURES**

Look carefully at the photograph of the Last Best West poster.

1. What **symbols** of Canada and Alberta can you see on this poster?
2. If you lived in another country, would this poster make you want to come to Alberta? Explain the reasons for your answer.

 UNDERSTANDING THE STORY

Read the section called "New Beginnings."

1. Compare and contrast what each person in this passage hopes life in Alberta will be like.
   (a) What changes in lifestyle are they expecting?
   (b) How do they feel about these changes in lifestyle?
2. Read the section called "First Impressions" on page 41. How did settlers feel about the changes in lifestyle after they arrived in Alberta?

New Beginnings

There are many different reasons why people chose to leave their homes and friends to move to Canada. Molly Hooper remembered that her family spent hours lying on the floor at home in England. They were looking at pamphlets and maps, dreaming of Canada. Her family sailed for Canada in 1911.

Madge Davison wrote, "Dad said that there could be no peace in Ireland, the old scars ran so deep. Canada won out as the **promised land**."

In 1913, Ned Butler of England wrote that a Canadian agent spoke in his home town and showed pictures of Alberta. "He told us of the wonderful opportunities that were there … Conditions were not so good [in England], so we decided to go."

In 1921, these Scottish settlers posed with a poem that they made up before leaving Scotland. A "crofter" was someone who rented a small farm. Why do you think they called the West their "Trail to Happiness?"

Karl and Emilia Bjorkgren left Sweden in 1891. They went to the United States, where Karl worked in a factory. Their daughter Elvira wrote that her father hated the factory. She said, "He longed for the open spaces and freedom of the land." So they moved to Alberta.

Many people in Europe had never heard of Canada. They had no idea where it was. In Eastern Europe, many people were not educated and could not read. Sifton sent agents to talk to the people there.

The word spread among the Ukrainians, Russians, and Romanians. A few settlers wrote back from Alberta that the agents' stories were true. Stefan Dragan was one of the Ukrainians who came to Canada. He wrote,

I had never lived nor worked on a farm. On leaving school I worked in a factory until I was called to the army where I served four years. I worked at odd jobs in the village and was married soon after leaving the army. I read the papers about Canada and after talking to others we organized a party of seven families to go there.

Getting There

Many people in Eastern Europe had to sell everything they owned to buy **fare** on the train and the ship. They had to travel across Europe to Hamburg, Germany, where the ships left for Canada. Most of the British immigrants left from Liverpool, England.

Few of the **immigrants** could afford comfortable rooms on the ships. They were often crowded into bunk beds. They slept on straw instead of mattresses.

These passengers on a ship called the Empress of Britain *are travelling to Canada in 1911. Ask your friends at school if they know anyone who came to Canada recently. How did he or she come here?*

Mayer Hoffer was 17 years old when he travelled to Canada in 1917. He wrote this about his trip:

On the third day I took sick and I was sick for 11 days. My rye bread went **moldy** *and we had to throw it away. The smell of the ship was so bad that I could not stand it. On the sixth day I asked to be taken up on deck for fresh air. On the seventh day I thought that I would never see land again!*

Mayer feared that he would become "food for the fishes," but he did arrive safely in Canada.

First Impressions

Once in Canada, the immigrants boarded a crowded train. Somewhere on the prairie the train would stop. They would get off and wonder where they were.

For settlers from Europe, the prairie was stranger than they ever imagined. Their first view of the prairie was often a shock. Many of them had never seen a land without trees.

Ivan Pylypiw, one of the first Ukrainians to reach Alberta, wrote,

Our people who left home with the world in their eyes did not have any idea where they were going.

The newcomers were afraid of getting lost or of getting caught in a prairie fire. Most missed the trees of their homelands and felt very lonely.

Lucy Johnson, who came from London, England, wrote,

Every time I gazed across the prairie, it looked the same to me . . . All I could see was sky and straw-coloured grass . . . and a few trees about every million miles.

Another settler wrote,

*We reached the homestead at last. I'll never forget the **desolate** feeling that came over me, when, with the contents of the wagon out on the ground, we sat on a box and looked around, not a sign of any other human **habitation** or a road leading to one to be seen, nothing but **bluff** and water and grass.*

Another settler wrote of his first impression in 1909:

*I will never forget the completely lost feeling I had as I stood there alongside all my worldly possessions on the bald-headed prairie. I was twenty years young and very much alone. I decided the first thing to do was to get something to eat, then I realized I had no water. I took a pail and started out. I wandered around through the hills and sure enough I found a **spring** of real good water. I filled my pail and started for home, but—where was it?*

Choosing a Homestead

Once they arrived, the newcomers' first task was to choose a homestead. The best land was along the rivers, where there would be a lot of water. Most of that good land was taken first. Some people looked for flat land that was ready to plow. Others tried to be close to a railway. Some, like the Ukrainians, chose land with trees and streams to remind them of home.

Many newcomers chose land close to people who spoke the same language or shared the same religion. They tried to settle where they would have neighbours to talk to and to rely on for help.

FINDING LAND

Sarah Roberts came to Alberta with her family in 1906. Her family came from the United States. They hoped to find a new farm in Canada. They spoke English and her father knew something about farming. He had heard that there was still good land available around Red Deer. He did not know, however, how to find it.

The Roberts family rode to Red Deer in a wagon. When they reached Red Deer, Sarah's father took her with him to the Land Office. He explained to her that the chart on the wall showed all the land that was still available. "There are lots of places with no name on them," she said. Her father told her that she was right but that much of the land could not be settled. It was set aside for the railway company. Some would be used to build schools.

Sarah's father decided that he could not choose land just by looking at a chart. He had better go and look for himself. He hitched up the wagon and the family headed for the town of Stettler. When they got there, they saw that the town was busy with other people looking for land. Sarah's father turned the wagon around and headed out onto the prairie.

After two days of driving, Sarah's family was tired. They stopped by the cabin of a young man named Barfield. Mr. Barfield invited the family to stay with him and rest for a while. The next

continued

continued

day, he took a stick and drew some lines on the ground. He explained to Sarah that the land was divided into sections. Each of these sections was divided into quarter sections, like dividing a pie into four pieces. Mr. Barfield told Sarah's father that he chose his land after spending many weeks looking around the area.

"Did you see any other good land around here?" Sarah's father asked.

"Yes," said Mr. Barfield, "on this part of Section 18." He drew another map in the dirt.

The next day, Sarah's father hurried back to Red Deer. He claimed the land on Section 10 and paid a small fee for it. The Roberts family had found a new home.

Building a Home

After they arrived on their land, the settlers had to build a house. Those who had money could afford to buy lumber or even a house kit. Those who were poor had to use what they could find: earth, grass, and logs. Sometimes the first home was just a dug-out in a slope or a bank.

Sod Houses

Sod is a mixture of earth and grass. A sod house is made with this mixture. Sod houses were built on the prairies where sod was the only building material available. These houses were cheap. The only cost was for windows, hinges, and perhaps boards for a door.

The sod was plowed up in long, straight **furrows** about 35 cm wide and 10 cm deep. Pieces of sod about 70 cm long were placed grass-side down, like bricks, to make thick, tight walls. Spaces were left for the door and windows. For the roof, boards or light poles

Homesteaders plowed up sod to make sod houses. They also used their plows to farm their land.

made from poplar trees were covered with hay, then with a layer of thinner sod. The law required settlers to build houses at least 5.5 m by 7.3 m.

The inside walls might be covered by paper or cloth, or plastered with a clay. Blankets or poles made walls. Curtains hung in the windows. One disadvantage of sod roofs is they leaked when it rained. One advantage is they were warm in winter and cool in summer.

The sod houses served very well as a first house. To visitors, they often looked as if they were growing right out of the prairie. Frank Roe wrote this about his family's sod house:

> *More than one visitor told us that when approaching the little home in stormy weather, he had no suspicion that he was close to a dwelling until he drew near enough to see the stovepipe above the roof.*

IN THEIR OWN WORDS
Frank Roe Tells Why He Decided to Build a Sod House

▼

"I realized that we were at the end of our journey, that this was to be our home, that if we wanted a house to cover us, a well for drinking water, it would all have to be the work of our own hands.

Our thoughts turned to the house. A cellar was dug, but we found that the cost of lumber would take all our money. Whatever would happen to us if we had nothing to buy food with in the winter ahead? So we decided to put up anything with four walls and a roof."

▲

IN THEIR OWN WORDS
James Rugg Describes How His Family Built a Sod House in 1905

▼

"The walls were built like laying bricks. The sods were cut about two feet long, were thirteen inches wide and four inches thick laid with grass side down. We had one rough door about six feet high which was difficult to fit into the sod walls. The roof was a lean-to type, there were three small windows. Being set in wide walls not much light could come in. Many cold days in winter frost would gather on the inside of the windows.

Poles with hay and sods on top were used for the roof over. One day my father and I had gone to the bush for wood. A thunder and wind storm came and the roof was lifted off and fell into a small garden alongside the house. On our arrival home in the afternoon we found mother unhurt in the kitchen without a roof overhead.

The stove was all the heating we had in the winter. Very many of the days and nights it froze in the house in spite of my getting up and putting wood in the stove many times during the night. The wind often blew through the cracks of the sod walls."

▲

Log Houses

Wherever wood was available, settlers made their first home from logs. With any luck the first houses were soon replaced by a wood frame or brick house with several rooms, glass windows, and **shingled** roofs.

IN THEIR OWN WORDS

Stefan Dragan Tells About His Log House

▼

❝When we arrived at the farm we had no shelter but a kind of tent made of brush. I had brought cheesecloth and put it around to keep out the mosquitoes and flies. We lived in this for a week or two while I built our first log house. I carried the poles from the bush on my shoulders. Walls were built, then poles laid across making ceiling and roof. This was finished by piling hay on the poles like the top of a haystack. There was no floor. We lived in this house four or five years. We then built a new and bigger house. We lived in this house for many years, then built a larger and better one which is still in use.❞

> **brush** - *bushes, shrubs*
> **cheesecloth** - *a thin, loosely woven, cotton cloth used to wrap cheese*

▲

Sod houses were often a family's first home in the West. Eventually, homesteaders built new homes out of wood. This photograph shows an old sod house and a new wooden house.

Children on the Farm

Children were expected to help their parents with chores on the farm. Many children did not go to school because they were needed at home. Their chores included helping to harvest the crops, and making butter.

IN THEIR OWN WORDS

Eric Lloyd Lists His Chores

▼

"Kids were limited to certain things, sawing the wood, feeding the pigs and taking the swill from the house to the pigs, cleaning up the yard, boy's work. When you weren't in school you could tramp a load of hay in the hay rack, help weed the garden and get in the cows. My parents saw to it that we did our work when we got home from school. When we finished our time was our own until bedtime.

One thing I detested was when mother felt it was churning day and I had to turn the churn and carry the water to wash the butter and do everything . . . except making the butter. It was anything but an entertaining afternoon."

---

swill - *a mixture of food scraps that is fed to pigs*
to tramp - *to trample or crush*
hay rack - *the area of a barn where the hay is stored*
to churn - *to make butter by beating and shaking cream in a container*

▲

Everyone on the farm helped. This boy is churning butter. List the other chores Eric Lloyd describes. Compare his chores to the ones you do.

Community and Co-operation

Homesteaders needed to co-operate with each other to survive. A **community** organized work parties (called "**bees**") to build a house or barn, to clear a field, or make a quilt. A community would build a school and hire a teacher, who then lived with various people in the community. Settlers worked together to build churches and roads. The roads brought **tradespeople** and small **industry.** These things made communities grow.

VERONIA'S STORY

The following is a true story about a young Romanian girl's experience from the time her family left Romania to come to Alberta.

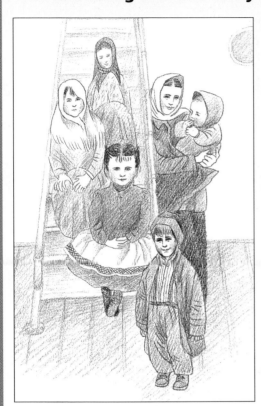

Like most newcomers, Veronia's family came to Canada on a ship. Veronia spent hours on the deck of the ship with other children.

My name is Veronia Kokotailo. I came to Canada with my parents in 1898. I was four years old. My father decided to leave our home village of Boian in Romania. Our family had lived there for as long as anyone could remember. Father decided to leave because we were very poor and there was no chance that life would get better for us.

We packed a few bags of clothing and bedding and some tools for farming. We crossed the ocean in a ship. I spent many hours sitting on the deck watching the older children play. Although we left behind the poverty of Romania, we also left behind many things dear to us. We missed our home, our relatives, our church, and our whole way of life. Most of all, I missed my friends.

We arrived in Alberta as summer began. The train carried us on the long trip from the sea to Edmonton. Father hired a wagon in Edmonton. We loaded it with our bags and the tools we brought. There was a shovel to dig, an axe to chop wood, and a hammer and saw to build a home. I crawled up behind Mother and watched Father hitch the horses to the wagon. We started the journey. The wagon rocked from side to side and I fell asleep.

Veronia's family hired a wagon to take them from Edmonton to their farm land.

continued

continued

Veronia's mother cut logs to build a log house.

When the wagon stopped I opened my eyes. All I could see was a forest of poplar trees and a bit of sky above. So this was our home in Canada!

Father and Mother cleared a space in the woods for our first home. Our house was nothing more than a hole dug into the ground. The roof was supported by poles, like a Native's tipi. The poles were covered with grass and sod. This kind of house was called a sod house.

When the sod house was finished, Father left us to find work in the town. He hoped to earn a few dollars to buy food for the winter. When he left, Mother sat down and cried bitterly. She said that living in a sod house made her feel like an animal living in a cave. She began to saw the fallen trees into logs. Without saying a word she worked day after day, cutting the logs and dragging them to a spot nearby. I watched in amazement as the logs formed four walls. She left a space for a door and put a window on one wall. She weaved willow branches over the top to form a roof. Before winter, we moved into our new log home. It seemed like a **luxury** after the sod house.

In that first summer we lived by eating berries, mushrooms, and roots that we gathered from the meadows nearby. Father returned from town with some flour and a bag of potatoes.

When Mother used the last handful of flour and put the last potato in the soup, we went hungry every day. Every night I cried and begged Mother for something to eat. We lived on wild mushrooms and chopped green grass. Finally Father returned again with a sack of flour and a pig's head.

In 1899 the wheat that Mother had planted grew golden in the sun. Father went again to find work. Mother harvested our first crop of wheat alone. She used a **sickle** to cut it. She tied it into **sheaves** and put it into **stocks** to dry. She also picked potatoes, peas, and beans from her vegetable garden, and stored them for the winter.

We are not so alone now. Other people from our homeland have settled around us. A small village has grown up nearby. We call it Boian, after the village that we left in Romania. Our people help one another. Mother showed some newcomers how to find wild mushrooms. She learned from others how to use animal fat to make soap. One family built a **grist mill** and Mother took our wheat there to grind it into flour. One of our neighbours catches fish in the river and brings them by for Mother to cook.

UNDERSTANDING THE STORY

Read "Veronia's Story."

1. Compare the experience of Veronia's family to experiences of other settlers in this chapter. What are the similarities and differences in their stories?

2. Imagine you are a member of Veronia's family. Write letters to your relatives in Romania. Tell about what you did when you first arrived in Alberta. Tell how you feel about being in Alberta. Would you say that they should join you?

GATHERING INFORMATION

1. (a) When did Canada first become a country?

   (b) Name the first four provinces in Canada.

2. Why was the foothill country in southern Alberta good for ranching?

3. Why did ranchers not want farmers to settle in the West?

4. How did Clifford Sifton advertise to get people to come and settle in the West?

5. After they chose a homestead, what did the newcomers have to do to survive life on the prairie?

6. How were "community" and "co-operation" important to the lives of homesteaders?

FURTHER STUDY

1. As a cowboy, describe a day in your life during a round-up.

2. Design a poster to advertise the land in the West. Be sure to make it attractive to someone who does not know what Alberta looks like.

3. Using a map of the world, find the countries that settlers came from.

4. In this chapter you have read what life was like for the homesteaders. Imagine that you are a homesteader. Write your own story. Remember to tell what country you are from and your reasons for coming. Write about the events of your first few months in the West.

5. Write a report on how the coming of homesteaders to the West changed the lives of the people already living there.

1861 *Father Lacombe founds Saint Albert*

1892 *The first Ukrainians come to Edna-Star*

1895 *The first Pole, Stanislaw Banach, comes to Alberta*

1906 *The first Japanese person, Kumataro Inamusu, comes to Alberta*

1887 *The first Mormons come to Alberta*

July 1, 1923 *Humiliation Day for the Chinese*

1894 *Jacob Shantz helps the first Mennonites come to Alberta*

1896-1921 *The Great Migration*

1911 *One in five Albertans had been born in Britain or the United States*

CHAPTER FOCUS

You have read in chapter 3 that Canada wanted people to settle in the West. You also read about what the newcomers hoped life in the West would be like. In this chapter you will learn more about the many groups of newcomers who came to Alberta.

How did the people who had already settled in Alberta feel about the newcomers?

Which groups of newcomers came to Alberta during the Great Migration?

What was it like for people to come to a place where there were no cities or farms?

How did newcomers help Alberta grow?

CHAPTER 4

THE GREAT MIGRATION

The Newcomers

In the late 1800s and early 1900s, many thousands of people said good-bye to their home countries, and made the long journey to Alberta. How those people came from all over the world to Alberta is a great story in Canadian history.

The first wave of newcomers came to Alberta in the 1880s and 1890s. They included French-speaking settlers, Mennonites, Icelanders, Mormons, and Hutterites. These people raised the population of Alberta to 73 000 in the year 1901.

You read in chapter 3 that Wilfrid Laurier became the prime minister of Canada in 1896. Laurier chose Clifford Sifton to find ways to make many more people want to come to Canada. Sifton was so successful that almost 3 million people came to Canada between 1901 and 1921. The second wave of newcomers came to Alberta at this time. They included the English-speaking settlers, Western Europeans, and Eastern Europeans. They raised the population to 588 000 in 1921. The time from 1896 to 1921 is called the **Great Migration**.

Each newcomer to Alberta met the challenges of making a home in a new land in his or her own way. Moving to a new land was also an experience shared with family and friends. When settlers cleared their own land and put up a house, they often helped others to do the same.

After a group of people settled an area, they began to develop a sense of community. They often shared their crowded homes with settlers who came later. Together they built roads, churches, and schools. They organized groups to entertain or to educate themselves. They organized dances, weddings, and picnics to break the boredom of hard work. Today we grow up in a society that is already made. The newcomers had to create their own society.

WORDS TO DESCRIBE THE MOVEMENT OF PEOPLE

Historians use three terms to describe the movement of people.

Migration is the movement of people from place to place. Migration can mean to or from a certain place.

Emigration means the movement of people *from* a certain place. We could say, for example, that the Scots emigrated from Scotland. They were emigrants.

Immigration means the movement of people *to* a certain place. We could say that the Scots immigrated to Alberta. They were immigrants.

Social Groups

A **social group** shares the same language, beliefs, and **customs**. Groups may be held together by the same language, by memories of their country of origin, or by religious beliefs.

Social groups were important in the time of the Great Migration. Members of a social group might share the same reasons for leaving their homeland. For example, many Ukrainians left Ukraine because there was not enough land for everyone there.

Each social group was different. For example, those groups who spoke English found it easier to set up a business or to work in the government. Those groups who spoke French fought to have their children taught in French.

Some groups, such as the Dutch, quickly learned to speak English. Others, like the Hutterites kept most parts of their daily lives separate from other people's. They kept their own language and style of dress. The reason that they came to Alberta was to keep their way of life. Most groups, such as the Ukrainians, mixed parts of their old way of life with the customs of their new homeland.

In this chapter, you will learn more about these groups and many others that came to Canada.

The First Groups of Newcomers

Only a few groups of settlers lived in Alberta before the Great Migration. Even after the railway was built, many people thought that Alberta was too dry for farming, too cold, and much too far away.

The first people to move to the West in large numbers already knew something about

Many different groups of people came to Canada because they were unhappy in their home countries. This group of Polish settlers are co-operating to build a place of worship at Skaro, Alberta in 1919.

Alberta. They knew how to survive conditions there. The groups who came to Alberta in the 1880s and 1890s include the French, Mennonites, Icelanders, Mormons, and Hutterites.

French-speaking Albertans

The French are the second-oldest group in Alberta, after the Native people. They came to Alberta in the fur trade as traders and **voyageurs**. Some of them married Native women. Their children became the new Metis nation in the West. You read about the Metis in chapter 2.

French was the first European language spoken in Alberta. Many places in Alberta have French words in them. Some examples are Lac la Biche, Bon Accord, and Beaumont.

In 1852, a Catholic priest named Father

Albert Lacombe came to Alberta from Quebec. In 1861 he founded a settlement near Edmonton which he named for his **patron saint**, Saint Albert. By 1885 more than half the population around Edmonton was French.

Father Albert Lacombe founded a French settlement called Saint Albert in 1861.

You read in chapter 2 that the Metis rebelled in 1885. After the Metis leader Louis Riel was hanged, many Metis moved from Manitoba and Saskatchewan to Alberta. Most Metis spoke French.

Soon, however, there were more English-speaking newcomers than French. They brought a very strong belief that English must be the only language used in the schools. They had fought this battle in Ontario and they fought it in Alberta. In 1892 the English **majority** passed a law stating that all students must be taught in English. Today, however, there are many French language courses and French schools in Alberta.

More French settlers came in the 1890s and settled in Morinville, Saint Paul, Bonnyville, and Falher. Almost all these French-speaking newcomers came from Quebec or from the United States. A few came from France.

Mennonites

The Mennonites are a religious group who follow the teachings of Menno Simons. Simons taught his followers that they must live and dress simply, and that they must live peacefully. The Mennonites were treated badly in Europe because they refused to fight in wars.

Mennonites were excellent farmers. The Canadian government wanted them to come to Canada. The government promised that if they came, they would not have to join the army. They could also have their own schools so that they could teach the Bible and the German language.

In 1894 Jacob Shantz helped many Mennonites move to Alberta. He and his family **founded** the town of Didsbury.

Today, some Mennonites continue to follow the old teachings. Many others have moved to the cities and live and dress as other Canadians do.

Icelanders

Iceland is a small island in the Atlantic Ocean. It is a land of volcanoes and **glaciers**. Icelanders first moved to the United States and later moved to Alberta. They travelled to Calgary by train, then walked for six days to the Red Deer River. They founded the town of Markerville.

The Icelanders faced the same difficulties as other newcomers. But the Icelanders were used to rough conditions. They knew how to hunt and fish. They raised sheep and made woollen clothing.

Icelanders brought a strong love of books and poetry. Stephan Stephansson was one of the leaders of their community in Canada. He wrote poetry and was one of the greatest Icelandic writers.

Stephansson wrote the following poem.

TOAST TO ALBERTA

Here veils of Northern Light are drawn
   On high as winter closes,
And hoary dews at summer dawn
   Adorn the wild red roses.
Sometimes the swelling clouds of rain
   Repress the sun's caresses;
But soon the mountains smile again
   And shake their icy tresses.

This photograph shows Stephan Stephansson's homestead in Markerville, Alberta. Stephansson is the man on the far left. He was born in Iceland in 1853 and moved to Canada in 1889.

 ## UNDERSTANDING THE PEOPLE

1. Choose one of the following people who are talked about in this chapter:
   - Father Albert Lacombe,
   - Jacob Shantz,
   - Stephan Stephansson, or
   - Charles Ora Card.
2. Find more information about the person you have chosen using another resource book. Explain to your class how the person helped shape Alberta.

Mormons

Mormons belong to the Mormon Church. It is also called the Church of Jesus Christ of Latter-day Saints. Their religious beliefs include keeping records of relatives who have died.

The Mormons moved from the eastern United States to the western state of Utah. Americans thought it was a crime for Mormon men to have several wives at once. Some of the Mormon men were put in jail.

In 1887, Charles Ora Card led the first Mormon settlers to what is now Alberta. The town of Cardston is named for him. Canadians did not approve of the Mormon marriages either. Soon the Mormons stopped the practice.

The Mormons are very skilled farmers. They developed Alberta's first irrigation system. Irrigation is a way to bring water to dry land. The water is brought by using ditches and sprinklers. Irrigation let the Mormons bring water to the dry land in southern Alberta.

Most of Canada's 113 000 Mormons live in southern Alberta today. Cardston is the site of Canada's first Mormon temple.

Hutterites

Hutterites are named for the religious leader Jacob Hutter. Their beliefs have changed little over the past 450 years. Hutterites believe that all property belongs to the group, not to individuals. They are pacifists. A pacifist is a person who tries to live peacefully and refuses to take part in wars. Hutterites dress and speak German like their ancestors.

Hutterites were treated badly in Europe because of their beliefs. They fled from one country to another and finally came to Canada. They settled in the prairies. Today there are about 20 000 Hutterites in Canada.

Hutterites are very successful farmers. They live on large farms called colonies. Each colony has about 13 families, about 85 people. When the population grows, the Hutterites form new colonies. There are now about 120 Hutterite colonies in Alberta.

Although some young people leave the colonies, most return. The traditional Hutterite way of life continues to survive today.

The English-speaking Newcomers

English-speaking immigrants came to Alberta in large numbers in the 1880s and 1890s. They came from Ontario, from Britain, and from the United States.

The Settlers from Ontario

People in Ontario showed an interest in Alberta even before it became part of Canada. So many people came from Ontario that they became the largest single group of people in Alberta. They came for land and for a new start. They also came to bring their ideas of what Canada should be to the West.

One of the first to come was Frank Oliver. He was the first newspaper publisher in Alberta. He went to Manitoba first and hired a cart to bring him to Fort Edmonton. There he set up the *Edmonton Bulletin*, which was Alberta's first newspaper. Oliver then went into politics. He helped to make Edmonton the capital city of Alberta.

Hutterites are a German-speaking group who came to Alberta. Hutterites dress like their ancestors and live on farming colonies.

Frank Oliver set up the first newspaper in Alberta. This is a photograph of the printing press he used to make his newspaper.

Settlers from Ontario had many advantages over other groups. They spoke English, which was the language of business and politics in Alberta. Many were also educated. Many of these settlers helped Alberta to become a province in 1905.

Some settlers from Ontario also brought some old **attitudes**. Some of the people wanted everyone to be like them. They wanted everyone to speak English. For example, they did not want French Albertans to have French schools.

James Lougheed was a classmate of Frank Oliver in Ontario. Lougheed moved to Calgary where he became a successful businessman. The prime minister chose him to enter the **Senate** in Ottawa. His grandson, Peter Lougheed, was premier of Alberta from 1971 to 1985.

Frederick Haultain was another successful newcomer from Ontario. He moved to Fort Macleod and became the leading politician in the West.

More than 50 000 people moved from Ontario to Alberta during the Great Migration. They settled on farms, on ranches, and in towns. In some parts of Ontario, there was wild enthusiasm to move to the West. The slogan in some towns was "All for the West. All aboard. Everyone must go to the Promised Land!"

The British

Over one million English, Scottish, and Irish people came to Canada between 1900 and 1914. (Together they are called **British**.) Many came to Alberta. In 1911 one in five Albertans had been born in Britain.

Some newcomers from England settled in ranching country in southern Alberta. A few were the younger sons of wealthy families. Because only the oldest son could **inherit** the family **estate** in England, some younger sons moved to western Canada. Many of these sons kept their old English lifestyle. They held formal balls and played English sports, like polo, cricket, and tennis.

Most British immigrants were workers from cities and towns. They had little or no experience in farming. Some tried farming, failed, and moved to towns to start businesses. They built many of the buildings, homes, and railways in early Alberta.

The British had a strong influence on early Alberta. Like some Ontario settlers, they believed Alberta should be English-speaking and Protestant. They were loyal to British traditions and tried to help Britain whenever it went to war. They also celebrated the birthday of the king or queen of England.

The Americans

By 1900 most of the free land in the United States had been settled. When Canada invited Americans to settle in the Canadian West, many came. Nearly 600 000 Americans moved to Canada between 1898 and 1914. In 1911 one in five Albertans had been born in the United States. In parts of southern Alberta one-half of the farms were owned by Americans.

Many American settlers came to Canada when most of the free land in the United States had been settled.

The Western Europeans

The largest groups of Western Europeans who came during the Great Migration were Dutch and German.

Dutch

The Dutch come from Holland. Holland is also called The Netherlands. From 1890 to 1914, Dutch immigrants moved to the Canadian West to homestead. They built settlements such as Monarch and Neerlandia in Alberta. Most were farmers. More came in the 1920s to work in construction and in factories.

Dutch settlers learned English, but they have tried to keep their religious traditions alive. Some Dutch religious groups have set up their own schools.

Germans

Few Germans who came to Canada had been born in Germany. Most were from other European countries. Some religious groups that came (such as Hutterites and Mennonites) also spoke German. From 1880 to 1900, thousands of German-speaking settlers came to the prairies. German communities in Alberta included Medicine Hat and towns between Calgary and Edmonton. By 1911, there were about 41 000 German-speaking newcomers in Alberta. Churches were important in the early German settlements.

In **World War I** (1914 to 1918), Britain and Germany went to war against one another. The war made English Albertans afraid of the German settlers. They believed that the

Germans wanted to help Germany in the war. The English Albertans would not let the Germans use their own language. They also took away the Germans' property.

Many more Germans came to Alberta in the 1950s and 1960s. Today, many Albertans are of German origin.

The Eastern Europeans

During the Great Migration, large numbers of people came to Canada from Eastern Europe. They included Ukrainians, Romanians, and Poles.

Ukrainians

Most Ukrainians lived under the rule of Russia or the **Austrian Empire** at the time of the Great Migration. Many were poor and lived on small pieces of land. Very few of them had even heard of Canada.

In 1891 two Ukrainians, Ivan Pylypiw and Vasyl Eleniak, visited Canada. They returned to Ukraine and encouraged others to follow them to Alberta.

The first Ukrainian settlement in Canada was Edna-Star, east of Edmonton in 1892. Ivan Pylypiw moved there after a German friend told him about it. In the next 20 years, about 170 000 Ukrainians came to Canada. By 1921, there were over 23 000 in Alberta. They settled in areas where they would be close to their friends and families.

Ukrainians kept many of their traditions. They celebrated their Christmas and weddings as they had done in Ukraine. They built many churches with onion-shaped domes to remind them of Ukraine.

Many parents wanted their children taught in the Ukrainian language. The government allowed Ukrainian to be taught at the end of the school day. Ukrainians kept their language and traditions alive. They had part-time schools, reading societies, and adult education groups.

Ukrainians lost some of their rights during World War I. Because many Ukrainians came from the Austrian Empire, many Canadians thought they would side with the enemies. A Ukrainian newspaper editor wrote in reply to this view:

> *For us Canada is first, we have sworn our loyalty to this country, and we do not see the reason why we have to be regarded as enemies.*

This group of Ukrainian performers came to Canada in 1918. How has this group continued to celebrate its customs?

Many more Ukrainians came to Alberta after the war was over. Many joined the early Ukrainians in the settlements around Edna-Star. Today, Edmonton has the largest number of people of Ukrainian origin in Canada. Many Ukrainian Albertans share their interest in Ukrainian language, food, dancing, and other activities with other Albertans.

Romanians

Romanians came from the same area of the Austrian Empire as many Ukrainians. Although their languages are different, Ukrainians and Romanians had many things in common. Both settled on farms in the same area of Alberta. Their clothing, music, dances, and art were similar.

The first Romanians came to Alberta in 1898. They founded the town of Boian, which they named after their home town in Romania. They were very poor when they arrived. Although many were hungry in the early days, they survived on their crops, wild mushrooms, roots, and berries.

By 1921 there were about 2000 Romanians in Alberta.

Poles

Poles come from Poland. Poland is a country in Eastern Europe. During the Great Migration many Poles left Galicia. Galicia was a poor area of Poland. The first Polish newcomer to Alberta was Stanislaw Banach. He arrived in Edmonton in 1895 with his wife and eight children. Soon, many other Poles followed.

The Polish settlers worked together to dig wells and build cabins. They borrowed horses and equipment from each other. The Catholic Church played a big part in their daily lives.

These Polish Canadians came together for a wedding in the 1930s. Their families came to Canada during the Great Migration.

The priest often helped the Poles with language problems. He advised the settlers on their problems and brought medicine to the sick.

Many Poles were miners who worked in Alberta's coal mines. They settled in Drumheller and Coleman. More than 7000 Poles lived in Alberta in 1921.

Caught Between Two Worlds

All immigrants are caught between two worlds. They are loyal to their old way of life, but they need to adapt to their new country.

Immigrants such as the Irish and Scots fled hunger in their countries. They left their homes with no thought of returning. Many others thought they would return home with money to help their families.

During the Great Migration, many English-speaking Albertans feared newcomers who spoke different languages. They did not understand the newcomers' religions. The

English-speakers believed that these people would not fit into their way of life. They feared the newcomers would change their lifestyles.

Many English-speaking Canadians thought they were better than others. This shocked many non-English-speaking newcomers. They had left their homes to be free in Canada.

Many newcomers returned home in disappointment, or moved on to the United States. From 1901 to 1911, for example, 1.8 million immigrants came into Canada, and 1 million people left. From 1911 to 1921, 1.6 million came, and 1.3 million left.

Europeans and Native People

Many newcomers, no matter where they came from, thought they were better than Native people. They tried to "save" the Native people by teaching them Christian beliefs. They stopped the Natives from practising their traditional ceremonies. They broke up Native families by making Native children attend schools far from home.

PREJUDICE AND DISCRIMINATION

Prejudice means to pre-judge, or to form an opinion before knowing the facts. Prejudice is usually a negative attitude toward other groups. The other group may be a different **race**, sex, religion, or from a different country.

Prejudice carries strong emotions, even hatred. It may be expressed through insults or jokes. It leads to unfair acts or violence.

While prejudice is a way of thinking, **discrimination** is a way of acting. Discrimination is an action that limits the freedom of others.

COMBATING PREJUDICE

Over the past 200 years, several powerful ideas have fought the view that certain groups are **inferior** because they are different. One is the idea that all people are created **equal**. They should be treated the same by the government and by the law.

Education helps to fight prejudice by helping people understand and accept differences. In Canada there are laws to stop people from acting on their prejudice.

RACISM

Racism is the belief that one race is better than others. For example, in the 1600s and 1700s, European countries took over much of the rest of the world. Many Europeans thought that their success meant that the white race was **superior**. Many Canadians believed this well into the 1900s. Some believe it today.

Racism can even be found in government. For example, the Canadian government made it difficult for Blacks, Chinese, Japanese, Jews, and others to come to Canada in the past.

White and Black

Slavery was not allowed in the United States after 1865. Even after that, Black people were discriminated against. Only the poorest jobs were open to them. Most were forced to live in separate areas from whites. They were not allowed in white people's churches, hotels, restaurants, theatres, or swimming pools. They received poor education because they were not allowed to go to schools for white children. Some moved to Alberta but were treated much the same there.

You read about John Ware in chapter 3. He was one of the first Blacks to move to Alberta from the United States. He was a skilled cowboy and owned his own ranch. Yet, when anyone stole a horse in Calgary, the police suspected him, just because he was Black.

Between 1908 and 1911, about 1000 Black Americans came to Alberta. They chose to live in **isolated** communities to avoid racism. The first group of Blacks settled about 100 kilometres west of Edmonton at Wildwood. The land was poor and there was no road, but the community survived. The people hunted and grew vegetables. They found work on the railways and built a Baptist church. They learned many skills from their Native neighbours.

Today the **descendants** of the original Black settlers are found in all areas of Alberta society.

Immigration Policy

Many English-speaking Canadians wanted people like themselves to come to Canada. They wanted British and American newcomers most. They **ranked** other newcomers on a scale according to how much they wanted them to come to Canada.

People from Northern and Western Europe were high on the scale. People from Central and Eastern Europe were lower on the scale. Many English-speaking Canadians did not want Blacks, Chinese, and Japanese people to come to Canada. These prejudices were a part of the Canadian government's immigration **policy**.

The Chinese built this arch in Edmonton in 1909. The sign on the arch tells the king of England that the Chinese are loyal to him.

Asian Newcomers

Asian newcomers to Canada included Chinese and Japanese people.

The first Chinese to come to Canada were brought by the Canadian Pacific Railway. The company needed men to build the railway through the Rocky Mountains. The Chinese did the most dangerous jobs and received very low pay. They were expected to return to China, but some stayed in Canada.

Some Chinese came to Alberta in the 1890s. Almost all settled in towns and cities. Many Chinese opened restaurants and laundries there. Many Canadians believed that the Chinese could never become part of Canadian society. The Canadian government refused to allow any more Chinese to come to Canada unless they paid a tax of $500. Very few could afford this amount of money.

As a result of the tax, the Chinese men could not bring their families to Canada. By 1921 there were 3500 Chinese in Alberta and only 200 were women. On July 1, 1923, the government passed a law preventing Chinese from entering Canada. Chinese Canadians remember that day as Humiliation Day. The law was cancelled in 1947.

The Chinese lived in their own part of town, called Chinatown. They supported one another and tried to keep their Chinese customs. A new wave of Chinese came to Alberta in the 1970s. This time Alberta welcomed them. There are now over 50 000 Chinese in Alberta.

The first Japanese person to settle in Alberta arrived in Calgary in 1906. His name was Kumataro Inamusu and he became the chef at the Alberta Hotel. Soon after, about 1000 Japanese came to work in the **sugar beet** industry. In 1907, Canada limited the number of Japanese who could come to Canada. This action was the result of racist feelings. By the 1940s there were only 540 Japanese in Alberta.

Japanese newcomers were not allowed to come to Canada again until 1967. Some of the later newcomers settled in Alberta, near Lethbridge and Edmonton. These newcomers brought many traditional Japanese skills, such as paper folding and flower arranging. Some helped young Japanese Canadians to learn Japanese arts, crafts, and language.

DISCUSSING THE ISSUES
ACCEPTING THE NEWCOMERS

Activities

1. What questions are these students asking? Write the questions in your own words.
2. Choose one of the answers the students give. With a partner, discuss why you think it is the best answer to the questions.

MULTICULTURALISM

Most Canadians today accept that different customs and beliefs from around the world add richness to Canadian life. The idea that Canadian society is made up of people with many different origins is called multiculturalism.

A New Society

Historians do not try to decide if the actions or beliefs of past generations were right or wrong. Each generation can only see the world according to its own experience. Part of the experience of Albertans is to live and work near people with many different origins.

Today, Canada has laws to protect people from the effects of racism and prejudice. Fewer people now hold the belief that they are better than other people because of their race or group. These changes have come about slowly. People continue to come from all over the world to Alberta.

Land of Opportunity

The Great Migration brought many groups of people to Alberta. Many became farmers. The world seemed eager to buy all the grain that these farmers could grow. Out of the mixture of peoples from all over the world, Alberta began to grow and change.

FURTHER STUDY

GATHERING INFORMATION

1. What does migration mean?
   (a) Why is the time from 1896 to 1921 called the Great Migration?
2. Who were the first groups of newcomers to settle in Alberta?
   (a) What languages did they speak?
   (b) What English-speaking groups came to Alberta in the 1880s and 1890s?
3. Who were the immigrants who came from
   (a) Western Europe?
   (b) Eastern Europe?
4. How did the different immigrant groups who settled in Alberta develop a sense of community?
5. What were some problems that some newcomers faced when they arrived?
6. Which of the groups that settled in Alberta found it easiest to fit into their new home? Why was it easiest for them?

1. Each of the groups that settled in Alberta brought its customs, language, and traditions. Choose one of the groups described in this chapter and write a report on its contributions to Alberta.
2. Create a timeline showing the Great Migration and the arrival of the different immigrant groups in Alberta.
3. Prejudice and discrimination were experienced by many newcomers to Alberta. Explain what these terms mean. Give examples of how prejudice and discrimination affected newcomers. Do you think prejudice and discrimination are still experienced today in Alberta?
4. Pretend you are a Native person living in Alberta during the Great Migration. Describe how you feel about the newcomers. Describe the changes the newcomers bring.

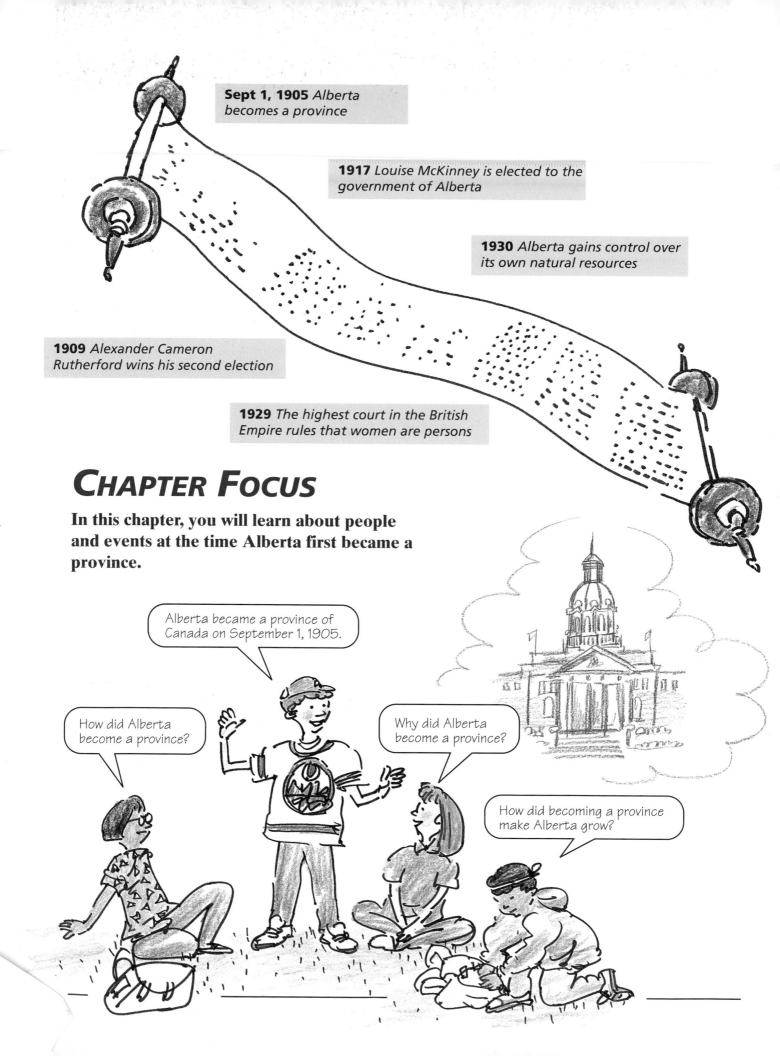

Sept 1, 1905 *Alberta becomes a province*

1917 *Louise McKinney is elected to the government of Alberta*

1930 *Alberta gains control over its own natural resources*

1909 *Alexander Cameron Rutherford wins his second election*

1929 *The highest court in the British Empire rules that women are persons*

CHAPTER FOCUS

In this chapter, you will learn about people and events at the time Alberta first became a province.

Alberta became a province of Canada on September 1, 1905.

How did Alberta become a province?

Why did Alberta become a province?

How did becoming a province make Alberta grow?

CHAPTER 5

BIRTH OF A PROVINCE

Opening Ceremonies

Alberta became a province of Canada on September 1, 1905. That day was filled with celebrations in the new **capital city** of Edmonton. The cannons boomed a salute which echoed through Edmonton's river valley. Thousands of people cheered. French and English Canadians, Cree, Stoney, and many others marched in a lively parade. They crowded around a stage draped with the **Union Jack**. They listened to the **governor general** of Canada. He said the following.

IN THEIR OWN WORDS

Governor General Earl Grey Makes a Speech

▼

"I consider it a great privilege to be able to take part as the representative of the King at the coming of age festivities of your people . . . the day which marks the addition of a new province to the Dominion of Canada."

representative - *a person chosen to speak or do something for others*
coming of age - *growing up*
Dominion of Canada - *the country of Canada*

▲

The Canadian prime minister, Wilfrid Laurier, was also present at the ceremonies. He spoke to newcomers to Alberta in his speech.

IN THEIR OWN WORDS

Prime Minister Wilfrid Laurier Speaks to Newcomers

▼

"We do not want any individual to forget the land of his origin . . . but let them give their heart, their soul, their energy to Canada."

▲

Wilfrid Laurier spoke to Albertans at the ceremony in which Alberta became a province.

The Jumping Off Point

Before Alberta became a province, it was part of the North-west Territories. It was run mostly by the Canadian government in Ottawa. The people living in the West had little control over their own territory's affairs.

For example, in 1904, the *Calgary Herald* newspaper complained that the Canadian government made a lot of money from selling land in the West. The government, however, would not give money to the North-west Territories when the West needed to build roads and bridges. If the West had its own provincial government, it could make its own decisions about how to spend money.

The settlers who came to the West wanted to make their own laws and decisions. Many of these settlers came from Ontario. Ontario was a province. It had its own provincial government to run its affairs. The settlers from Ontario wanted the North-west Territories to be a province with its own government.

You read about Frederick Haultain in chapter 4. He was one of the strongest voices demanding that a new province be created. He said,

We have now reached the jumping off place, and can go very little farther without becoming a province.

Frederick Haultain worked hard to have Alberta become a province.

Prime Minister Laurier disagreed with Haultain. He did not believe that the time was right to create a new province. He thought there were too few people in the West. He also was not sure how many new provinces to divide the West into.

One Province or Two?

Some people thought that the North-west Territories should become part of British Columbia. Many people in the territories, however, felt that they had nothing in common with that province.

Haultain argued that the territories should become one large province. This huge province could be as powerful as Ontario or Quebec. Finally, Laurier decided that two provinces would be better than one. This decision seemed to suit the people in the West as well. One province became Alberta and the other became Saskatchewan. They were roughly the same size.

A Name for the New Province

The name "Alberta" had already been given to part of the North-west Territory. Alberta was named after Princess Louise. Alberta was one of her middle names. She also gave her name to Lake Louise. Princess Louise was the daughter of Queen Victoria of England.

IN THEIR OWN WORDS

Princess Louise Writes to a Man in Lethbridge in 1924

You are perfectly correct in your belief that the beautiful, sunlit and prosperous Province of Alberta was named after me by my husband, the Marquis of Lorne, when he was Governor-General of Canada . . . He decided to call it after my last name, Alberta, of which he was very fond. Indeed, he mostly called me by it, or shortened it to Alba.

I am intensely proud of this most beautiful and wonderful Province being called after me, and that my husband should have thought of it . . . I was named Alberta after my father [Prince Albert].

Princess Louise Alberta gave her names to a province and a famous lake in the Rocky Mountains.

Who Would Own the Land and Natural Resources?

One of the greatest powers that a province of Canada has is ownership of its land and **natural resources**. A province with many natural resources such as timber, fish, or gold, is rich. The people who live there will have jobs. The first four provinces of Canada (Ontario, Quebec, New Brunswick, and Nova Scotia) were given ownership of their land and resources in 1867.

When the prairie provinces were created, (Manitoba in 1870, Alberta and Saskatchewan in 1905), the Canadian government did not give them ownership of their own land and resources. The Canadian government said that it needed the money from these lands to pay for railways and bringing newcomers to the West.

Alberta finally gained control of its own land and resources in 1930. Now, Alberta receives money from the sale of oil and gas in the province.

In Alberta today, the provincial government is the largest owner of natural resources. Oil, mineral, and forest companies in Alberta rent land from the provincial government.

Which City Would Be the Capital?

After the politicians decided to create two provinces, one big question remained. What would be the capital city of Alberta?

Being the capital city can be very important to a city. A capital brings **prestige**, many jobs in the government, and a magnificent new capital building.

Several cities in Alberta wanted to become the capital. The real contest, though, was between the two largest cities, Calgary and Edmonton.

CALGARY'S CLAIM

The Calgary newspaper said that Calgary was clearly the best choice for Alberta's capital. The newspaper pointed out that Calgary had a larger population than Edmonton.

R.B. Bennett was a Calgarian who later became prime minister of Canada. Before Alberta became a province he said,

> We should remember that if we become a province, Calgary would become the capital. In [Eastern Canada] Calgary is always spoken of with praise as an **enterprising** city with fine buildings and energetic citizens. In every sense of the word we are entitled to become the capital.

EDMONTON'S CLAIM

Edmonton was just as sure that it would be the capital. Its newspaper said,

> Edmonton should from its central position and the convenience of its railway system, and with its great . . . agricultural **prospects**, become the capital of the province.

Edmonton became the capital city of Alberta. Here, the new Alberta legislature building is being built in Edmonton. The government of Alberta meets in this building.

There were good reasons to choose Calgary, and good reasons to choose Edmonton. The decision was made in Ottawa. Frank Oliver and Peter Talbot worked hard to make Edmonton the capital. Edmonton was finally chosen.

The First Election

Now that Alberta was a province, it had the right to elect its own government. The leader of Alberta's government is called the premier.

In 1905, there were two **political parties** in Alberta. They were the Liberal Party and the Conservative Party. The Conservative Party chose R.B. Bennett to lead them. He was born in New Brunswick. He had four goals in life: to become a millionaire, to become premier of Alberta, to become prime minister of Canada, and to be made an **English Lord**. He achieved all of these goals except that he never became premier of Alberta.

Alexander Cameron Rutherford was a lawyer who became the first premier of Alberta. Why was he forced to resign five years later?

The Liberal Party chose Alexander Rutherford to lead them. He had grown up in Ontario and was now a successful lawyer in Edmonton. In the first election, he became Alberta's first premier.

More Railway Fever

The people of Alberta wanted their new government to keep the province growing. They thought the only sure way to make this happen was to keep building more railways. The people of Edmonton wanted to connect their city with northern Alberta.

In 1909 there was another election. Rutherford promised that if he won this election, he would build three new railways: one to Peace River, another to Fort McMurray, and another to Athabasca Landing. He won the election.

The three new railways began to be built a year later. Some Albertans began to wonder if people in government were giving railway business to their friends. Some people believed that Rutherford had been doing this. Rutherford resigned and Arthur Sifton became premier. This was Alberta's first scandal.

ALBERTA'S FIRST PREMIER

Alexander Cameron Rutherford was born near Osgoode, Ontario, in 1857. He was a lawyer working near Ottawa until 1895. Then he moved to Edmonton. In 1905 he became the first premier of Alberta. He belonged to the Liberal Party.

Rutherford wanted a public education system and a public telephone system. These systems are called "public" because they offer a service to everybody. The government pays for the service.

He also wanted to build more railways. In 1910 he was forced to resign because of a **scandal**. He was later found innocent.

Rutherford's fine library of Canadian books now belongs to the Rutherford Library at the University of Alberta.

WOMEN GET THE VOTE

Men began to vote in elections in Canada in 1791. For more than 100 years, only men could vote or be elected to serve in the government. Most men and women believed that politics, law, and medicine were men's work.

In the 1800s, some Canadian women challenged this idea. They organized to bring about changes. For example, they wanted women to be paid better wages for their work. These women, however, found that they could not make many changes because they could not vote. They decided to try to get the right to vote.

Change came slowly until Nellie McClung arrived in Winnipeg in 1911. She was a fiery speaker who worked for women's rights. By this time, many men supported women's right to vote.

During World War I, thousands of men joined the army. While the men were away, thousands of women did men's jobs, like working in factories. Other women risked their lives in the war as doctors or nurses. Women proved they were equal to men.

Finally, women won the right to vote in Alberta in April 1916. Women first voted in elections for the government of Canada in September 1918.

This woman served in World War I as an ambulance driver.

Emily Murphy helped change attitudes towards women. She believed women were equal to men.

Women in the New Province

Emily Murphy

Emily Murphy was born in Ontario and moved to Alberta in 1907. She wrote several books under the name "Janey Canuck." Murphy worked hard to improve the lives of women and children. Largely because of her, the Alberta government passed a law in 1911 protecting a wife's right to a share in her husband's property.

Murphy also worked to gain women the vote. In 1916 she became police magistrate for Edmonton and then Alberta. A magistrate is a person who hears and decides cases in a law court. Murphy was the first woman to hold such a post in the **British Empire**.

On Murphy's first day as a magistrate in court, a lawyer told her that she was not a "person" according to the law. The lawyer said this because the **British North America Act** of 1867 stated that women were not "persons" by law. Women could not be chosen for positions in government, such as the **Senate**, because they were not "persons." Murphy then began a long campaign to have women declared "persons." This issue became known as the "Persons Case."

Murphy and four other Alberta women became known as "The Famous Five." The other women were Henrietta Edwards, Louise McKinney, Nellie McClung, and Irene Parlby. They worked together and took the Persons Case to the highest court in the British Empire. In 1929 the court ruled that women were indeed persons.

Louise McKinney

Louise McKinney came to Alberta from Ontario. She was one of the "Famous Five" who fought to have women recognized as "persons." In 1917 she was elected to the government in Alberta. She was one of the first women elected in Canada. She served in government until 1921.

Nellie McClung

Nellie McClung was another of the "Famous Five." She grew up on a homestead in Manitoba. She started school when she was 10 years old. In 1908 McClung published her first novel, called *Sowing Seeds in Danny*. It was about a small town in the West. The book sold well across Canada.

McClung worked for women to get the vote. When she moved with her family to Edmonton, she continued the work. She was elected to the government of Alberta in 1921. She served until 1926.

 ## UNDERSTANDING THE PEOPLE

Read the stories about Emily Murphy, Louise McKinney, and Nellie McClung.

1. What did these three believe about women?
2. How did the work of these women affect the lifestyles of Albertans and Canadians?

Looking Ahead

Alberta would continue to grow after becoming a province. The railway would cause new towns to form. Some towns would become cities. Natural resources, such as coal and oil, would also be important to the success of the new province.

 ## GATHERING INFORMATION

1. What happened to the North-west Territories in 1905?
2. What were Sir Wilfrid Laurier's reasons for not wanting Alberta to become a province?
3. How did Alberta get its name?
4. How was it decided where the capital of Alberta would be? Do you think this was a fair decision?
5. Women and men shaped the history of Alberta. Name the women mentioned in this chapter. What were their contributions?
6. What did Wilfrid Laurier mean when he asked newcomers to Alberta to give "their heart, their soul, their energy to Canada"?

 ## FURTHER STUDY

1. Choose three towns or cities in Alberta. Research how these towns or cities got their names.
2. When the prairie provinces were formed, the Canadian government did not give them control over their natural resources. This caused **conflict**.

   (a) Why do you think control over natural resources is important to provinces? You may want to read ahead to chapter 8 to help answer this question.

   (b) Does conflict over Alberta's natural resources still occur today? Read some current newspaper articles to find out.

1874 *Mining begins near Lethbridge*

1883 *Workers near Medicine Hat find natural gas by accident*

1883 *The railway arrives in Alberta*

1904 *Edmonton becomes a city*

1893 *Calgary becomes a city*

June 1914 *The Hillcrest mine disaster occurs*

May 1914 *Workers find oil and gas at Turner Valley*

CHAPTER FOCUS

Towns and industry in Alberta began to grow as the population grew. In this chapter, you will read how railways and natural resources promised to make Alberta a wealthy province in the early 1900s.

I have been on a bus and on a streetcar, but never on a railway. Why does everyone say that the railway was so important to Alberta?

In the movies, old trains use coal for fuel. Where did the coal come from? How was coal a part of Alberta's past?

Every town that I have ever visited in Alberta has a railway station. Is that how the towns and cities got their start?

Today, cars and many machines use oil and gas. How were these natural resources important in Alberta's history?

CHAPTER 6

RAILWAYS, INDUSTRY, AND THE GROWTH OF CITIES

In chapters 3 and 4, you read that hundreds of thousands of settlers moved to the West during the Great Migration. These settlers built houses, plowed the soil, and harvested their wheat.

At the same time, small towns appeared on the prairie.

 **UNDERSTANDING THE STORY**

Read the story called "A Young Boy's Life in Strathmore in 1917" on the following page.

1. Write a paragraph describing life in a small town.
2. Name some ways small towns served the people of Alberta.
3. Was the railway important in a small town? Explain your answer.

A YOUNG BOY'S LIFE IN STRATHMORE IN 1917

In the following story, a young boy describes Strathmore, Alberta in 1917.

Except for the trees, Strathmore is a pretty ordinary prairie town. On my way to school, I count all the brick buildings. The total never comes to more than ten. The Bank of Montreal is the biggest one. Main Street cuts right through the middle of town and disappears into the prairie. Some of the side streets are dirt trails. There are wooden sidewalks to keep your feet dry when the rain turns the streets to mud.

Many people still use horses to pull their carriages and their farm equipment. The blacksmith has a shop on Main Street. He replaces the horses' metal shoes and fixes the broken wheels. He heats the metal at an open fire. I wave at him when I pass by.

Strathmore is small, but it is an important place to the farmers who live in our area. They need a place to bring the wheat that they grow. Here they can load it onto the railway cars and ship it to markets all over the world. They can buy food and tools and equipment here. They can put their money in the bank. They can come here to talk with their friends.

If you come to Strathmore, the first things that you will see are the grain elevators. This is where the farmers store their grain until the railway trains come to take it away. Some of the elevators are painted bright colours. One is covered in shiny metal and shines brightly in the sun.

Our town depends on the railway. Every day my friends and I rush down after school to watch the trains arrive. Sometimes we meet people we know. Other times we just go to see the people who run the trains. The engineer, who drives the train, waves from his cab in the locomotive. The fireman, who shovels the coal into the hot furnace, wears a kerchief around his neck to catch his sweat. His striped overalls are black with coal dust.

One train comes from the east and another comes from the west. The trains drop off passengers, goods, mail, and newspapers. The conductor then checks his watch. It is his job to keep the train on time. At the exact second, he signals the engineer to start. He shouts, "All Aboard!" The whistle blows and the train begins to move, slowly at first, then quicker, and soon it disappears onto the flat prairie.

ORIGINS OF THE RAILWAY

The first railways were built to carry coal from mines. The rails allowed wagons carrying coal to run over very rough ground. These first railway cars were pulled by horses.

Later, engines that ran on steam power pulled many heavy cars across any kind of land. This kind of engine was called a locomotive. In Canada, railways moved goods and people in the winter, when the rivers were frozen. Railways also worked in the spring, when roads were muddy.

The railway joined Canada from the Atlantic Ocean to the Pacific Ocean.

Like every prairie town, Strathmore depended on the railway. What means of transportation do most Alberta towns rely on today?

READING PICTURES

Study the picture of Strathmore.

1. List the parts of a prairie town that you can see.
2. Why did prairie towns grow near railways?

Strathmore was one of hundreds of prairie towns that sprang up quickly. A town was a meeting place between the farmers and the outside world. It was a place where farmers could ship grain, visit the bank, buy food, lumber, clothing, tools, wagons, and other things.

One hundred years ago, the only permanent settlements were fur trading posts, such as Fort Edmonton and Fort Chipewyan, and police posts, such as Fort Macleod and Fort Calgary.

The Railway Arrives in Alberta

Like Strathmore, most towns in Alberta are located on a railway line. The railway was very important to life in the West. Towns formed wherever railway stations were built. When settlers heard where a railway station was to be built, they put up tents and waited. The railway company often tried to keep the location of a station secret. The company was afraid that everyone would rush to buy land, and fights would occur.

The Canadian Pacific Railway (CPR) arrived in Alberta in 1883. Some settlers guessed that it would have to cross the South Saskatchewan River. The settlers put up their tents there. The CPR did build a railway bridge and a station at that spot. This is how the town of Medicine Hat was formed.

The Railway Reaches Calgary

The railway went farther and farther west. It finally reached Fort Calgary in 1883. Fort Calgary was a small fur trading post. Before the railway arrived, about 100 people lived around Fort Calgary. They were Native people, fur traders, and members of the North-West Mounted Police.

The CPR decided not to build a railway station next to Fort Calgary. Instead, the CPR built a station one kilometre farther west. The storekeepers at Fort Calgary packed up and moved their buildings to the new location.

The Railway Reaches Edmonton

The people in Fort Edmonton wanted the railway to come north. Fort Edmonton was important to the fur trade although only 263 people lived there.

Life changed at Fort Calgary when a railway station was built nearby in 1883. What were trains used for in the past? What are they used for today?

The CPR built a railway from Calgary north towards Edmonton in 1891. The railway, however, did not go all the way to Edmonton. Instead, it stopped before crossing the North Saskatchewan River. A new town then started on the south side of the river.

You will learn more about Calgary and Edmonton later in this chapter.

Into the Rocky Mountains

The railway pushed westward into the foothills and the Rocky Mountains. In the mountains, three railway workers made a discovery. They smelled a strong odour of **sulphur** coming from the side of a mountain. They found **hot springs** that brought up water from underground. Many people believe such hot springs can cure sickness. The workers quickly tried to open a business to attract tourists.

In 1887, the Canadian government created Banff **National Park** to protect the mountain

area. The CPR opened the Banff Springs Hotel the very next year. Soon tourists, artists, and writers came to Banff from all over the world. Banff is still a favourite holiday area.

Complaints About the Railway

The West soon outgrew its railway. The CPR could not keep up with all the people, grain, and supplies it had to carry. Many people complained that the CPR charged too much money for its services. The Canadian government convinced the CPR to lower its **rates** in 1897, but the railway remained unpopular in Alberta.

The Canadian Northern Railway and the Grand Trunk Pacific Railway were two new railway companies that formed in the West. They competed with each other and the CPR. They learned, however, that while there was too much work for one railway, there was not enough work for three.

After World War I, the Canadian government took control of both the Canadian Northern Railway and the Grand Trunk Pacific Railway. The government joined the two companies to form the Canadian National Railways (CNR).

The railway brought the first tourists to the Rocky Mountains. The new Banff Springs Hotel was a comfortable place to stay.

When Coal Was King

In the early 1900s, a German businessman named Martin Nordegg went looking for coal in the foothills of the Rocky Mountains.

IN THEIR OWN WORDS
Martin Nordegg Finds Coal

▼

"Continuing our way, we came to the Bighorn River . . . Travelling on the east bank of the stream, we reached a beautiful double waterfall, and we decided to make a longer stay there in order to explore the country.

We walked along the river. Suddenly Dowling stopped and showed me on the other bank long horizontal black banks in the creamish rock.

"Is that coal?" I asked.

"No, that is shale. But below we are sure to find coal. This will be our first coal field."

Dowling placed two men at the side of the hill with orders to start driving a tunnel.

In the afternoon . . . one of the men came running down and brought a chunk of coal. There was great excitement.

"That is surface coal. It will get harder and harder the farther we go in." He threw it on the log fire, and immediately it started burning with a red flame."

> **horizontal** - *parallel to the horizon, level*
> **shale** - *rock made from mud or clay*
> **driving** - *digging*
> **surface coal** - *coal found close to the top of the ground. Surface coal is softer than coal found farther below ground.*

▲

Martin Nordegg was proud of his discovery. He later wrote:

> *To think that I had found it myself . . . Is it surprising that I could not find any sleep that night? I was lying now on the very ground where in the future a large coal mine was to operate, where hundreds of men would work, where I would build a town with pretty houses.*

Nordegg did build a town, which was named for him.

HOW COAL FORMS

Millions of years ago, the **climate** of Earth was warm and moist. Many forests were like thick, swampy jungles.

The plants stored up **energy** from the sun, then died. The dead plants became buried, crushed, and heated within the Earth. Over millions of years they slowly turned to coal. The slower this process was, the richer the coal became.

The story of the coal industry in Alberta is much less known than the stories of the ranchers and homesteaders. It is an important part of Alberta's history.

Coal was discovered in southern Alberta in 1793. Sometimes travellers used it to burn in campfires. Now the railways needed tonnes of coal. The engines that drove the railway locomotives ran on steam power. The **fuel** that the engines used to produce steam was coal. After 1900, the demand for coal increased. Homesteaders used coal to heat their homes. Industry needed it to provide energy for factories.

People came from all over the world to mine coal in Alberta. Coal was used to run trains and factories, and to heat homes.

The Crow's Nest Pass

The earliest coal mines were near the main line of the Canadian Pacific Railway, and the new Crow's Nest Pass Railway. By 1914, 8000 people lived in the Crow's Nest Pass area, in southwestern Alberta.

Two of the largest towns in the area were named for Americans who had set up coal mines there. Frank was named for H.L. Frank and Hillcrest was named for C.P. Hill. Coleman was the largest town in the area. Workers came from all over the world to work in the mines. They came from Britain, Italy, France, Belgium, Russia, and Poland.

Lethbridge: Coal Mining Town

Lethbridge was one of Alberta's most important coal mining towns. Mining began there in 1874. But the mines were not very big until the Canadian Pacific Railway was built in the 1880s.

Most of the miners worked to make enough money to live somewhere else. Often they saved enough to buy a farm.

The coal mined at Lethbridge was used mostly to heat homes. Lethbridge was a big town in the winter because coal was needed at that time of the year. The town would be full of miners. But it was a small town in the summer because the mines were not busy then.

A BOY'S EXPERIENCE IN A COAL MINE NEAR LETHBRIDGE

I am 12 years old and I have worked in the coal mine for 8 months now. I am getting used to it, but some of the other boys have a hard time. We hardly ever get a breath of air during the whole ten hours that we work.

In some parts of the mine the water is ankle deep and you get soaking wet. Even when it is too wet to dig the coal, you can't go home. You have to wait until your **shift** is over.

In the winter, the airways freeze and cut off the supply of air to the mine. The miners tell me to crawl in there and chop the ice. I almost freeze. If I come out to get warm, they will fire me. I see some of the boys spit up coal dust.

Several of the boys cannot speak English. They should be at school instead of working in the coal mine.

In the Mines

Coal mining was a difficult job for workers. Coal miners were not paid much money, and they had to work in uncomfortable conditions. Even 12 and 13-year-old children worked in the mines before World War I.

 UNDERSTANDING THE STORY

Read the section called "Disaster in the Mines."

1. With a partner, find out about coal mines in Alberta and other parts of Canada today.
   (a) Are there many coal mines in Alberta today? Name some places in Alberta and Canada where there are coal mines.
   (b) Are coal mines safer to work in today than they were in the early 1900s? Give reasons for your answer. Ask your librarian to help you find information on the Westray disaster in Nova Scotia in 1992.

Disaster in the Mines

Coal mining is dangerous. Underground coal mines can cave in because the rock around the coal is soft and weak. Methane gas is often present in coal mines. This kind of gas can cause deadly explosions.

The worst coal mine disaster in Canada happened at Hillcrest, Alberta in 1914. Early on the morning of June 19, 1914, everyone in Hillcrest heard three blasts on the mine whistle. This sound told them that a disaster had occurred.

Huge clouds of smoke came from the coal mine. People filled the roads to Hillcrest to see what happened. Hundreds of worried women and children waited to hear some news of their loved ones who worked in the mine. Explosions in the mine killed 189 men. This was the worst mining disaster in Canadian history.

Alberta had some of the most dangerous coal mines in the world. Another 10 miners died at Coleman in 1926. Sixteen died at Coalhurst in 1935, and 29 died at Nordegg in 1941. More than 1200 miners lost their lives in Alberta mines from 1904 to 1963.

The Hillcrest mine disaster was the worst in Canadian history.

The Discovery of Oil and Gas

In 1883, some railway workers were drilling for water near Medicine Hat. Suddenly something shot out of the ground and into the air. It burst into flames and blew up the water drilling rig. This is how natural gas was discovered in Alberta. Soon the town of Medicine Hat was using gas to light street lamps.

The biggest discovery of oil and natural gas in Alberta was at Turner Valley. Turner Valley is located southwest of Calgary. The discovery was made on May 14, 1914. Very quickly, 500 oil and gas companies formed in Calgary. These companies looked for more oil and gas. Nearly everyone put their money into one of these companies. They hoped to become rich.

PETROLEUM

Petroleum is the remains of plants and animals that lived millions of years ago. When they died, these plants and animals sunk to the bottom of the sea and became buried. These fossil remains turned into petroleum.

If petroleum is solid, it is either coal or bitumen. If petroleum is liquid, it is either oil or natural gas.

Petroleum is occasionally found seeping out of rocks. We usually get petroleum by drilling deep wells into the rock.

Oil sometimes looks like a thin, colourless liquid. Sometimes it is a heavy, black, gummy substance that looks like tar.

Natural gas is a colourless, odourless gas. It is often found together with oil. Much of the natural gas found in Alberta contains hydrogen sulphide and is called "sour" gas. This poisonous, bad smelling gas is dangerous and must be removed before the natural gas can be used.

Bitumen is also known as tar. It is a dark brown to black mixture. It is called tar sand or oil sand when it is found mixed with sand. It is very difficult and expensive to turn bitumen into useful oil.

Most petroleum needs to be prepared with special methods before it can be used.

THE OIL AGE

The use of oil in Canada grew as more and more people bought automobiles. In 1905 there were only about 500 cars in Canada. In 1915 there were more than 60 000. More and more gasoline was needed to fuel cars and trucks. Gasoline is made from oil.

Oil is easier to handle than coal because oil is liquid while coal is solid. Oil is the energy behind automobiles, trains, airplanes, and other vehicles.

Natural gas and oil were discovered at Turner Valley in 1914. Workers built this well to get the oil and gas from the ground.

Turner Valley produced enough oil and gas to supply the needs of Calgary until 1920. But the valley had supplied smaller amounts of oil and gas than everyone had expected. Almost everyone who had rushed to spend money on looking for oil and gas lost it all.

No one knew at the time that there was more oil and gas only 20 or 30 metres farther down in the ground. This oil and gas was not discovered until the 1920s and 1930s. Then, Turner Valley became Canada's first great oil field. Many people came to the oil field to work there.

In 1947, explorers found another oil field at Leduc, south of Edmonton. This discovery changed the history of Alberta forever. Alberta became Canada's leading producer of oil and gas. **Pipelines** in Alberta now carry the oil and gas to eastern Canada and to the United States.

You will learn more about Alberta's oil industry in chapter 8.

A Tale of Two Cities

Between 1901 and 1914, Edmonton and Calgary grew from small towns to **prosperous** cities. They grew faster than any other cities in Canada.

GROWTH OF CITIES IN ALBERTA

CITY	1881	1891	1901	1911	1921
Calgary	100	3876	4392	43 704	63 305
Edmonton	263	700	2626	31 064	58 821
Lethbridge	—	—	2072	9035	11 097
Medicine Hat	—	—	1570	5608	9634

This table shows the population of Alberta's cities from 1881 to 1921. Which city grew the fastest?

Edmonton

The North Saskatchewan River goes through Edmonton today, creating a large river valley. Native people came to this valley for at least a thousand years before the Europeans arrived. The riverbank was an excellent source of **quartzite**, which the Natives used to make stone tools.

THE FUR TRADE

European fur traders came to the area in 1795. The Hudson's Bay Company built Fort Edmonton here. The fort became the most important fur trading post in the West.

After the fur trade ended, Edmonton continued to be an important stop for people taking supplies to northern Alberta. These people were bringing goods such as food, tools, and building materials to farms and settlements in the north. Edmonton began to grow in the 1870s when the first settlers arrived to farm the surrounding land.

HOPES DELAYED

In 1875 there were high hopes in Edmonton. The railway planned to pass through the area. Already there were signs of the modern world in Edmonton. In 1879, a **telegraph** office was opened. Soon there was a post office, and Frank Oliver started the first newspaper in Alberta, called the *Edmonton Bulletin*.

The CPR, however, announced that the railway would go through Calgary instead of Edmonton. The people of Edmonton were surprised. In 1883 the railway reached Calgary and made that town prosper. Meanwhile, Edmonton's growth fell behind.

In 1891, the railway came as far as the south side of the North Saskatchewan River. Edmonton, however, was on the north side of the river. The CPR did not want to build a railway bridge across the river to Edmonton. Instead, the CPR started a new town on the south side of the river, called South Edmonton. (It was later renamed Strathcona.)

John Walter was one of the first people to settle on the south side of the river. He came from Scotland in 1870. He built a **sawmill** in south Edmonton. He also built boats and sleighs, and two **ferries** to move people from one side of the river to the other. He was one of the richest men in town until 1915, when a flood ruined his mill.

In 1897 Edmonton got a boost from the **Klondike Gold Rush** in the Yukon. Thousands of gold miners stopped off in Edmonton to buy supplies for their journey to the Yukon. The route the gold miners took to the Yukon was called the Klondike Trail. Some of the gold miners stayed in Edmonton and looked for gold along the river. Tom Clover was one person who found gold there. One of Edmonton's neighbourhoods is named for him.

As the population grew, coal mines also opened all along the river bank.

CAPITAL CITY

Edmonton became a city in 1904. The next year was the biggest in its history. In 1905, Alberta became a province and Edmonton became its capital. The Canadian Northern Railway also arrived that year. The Grand Trunk Pacific Railway arrived in 1909. Now Edmonton was as great a railway centre as Calgary. Workers were busy building a new government building and several fancy new hotels. More and more settlers passed through on their way to find homesteads.

This picture shows Edmonton in the making. The High Level Bridge would soon carry the railway across the river valley. The new legislature building in the distance would be a home for the government of Alberta. Compare this picture of Edmonton to the one on page 71.

In 1912, Edmonton and Strathcona united. The next year the High Level Bridge connected the north and south river banks. It was the fourth largest bridge in Canada at the time. The total population of Edmonton now was about 45 000.

Edmonton was on its way to becoming a big city. It was a centre of business, government, and education. It was, as it had been in fur trade days, the Gateway to the North.

In the 1920s Edmonton had an important airfield for a new industry — airplanes. In the 1930s thousands of people passed through Edmonton on the way to mines at Great Bear Lake and Yellowknife.

Since the 1940s, Edmonton has been one of Canada's two or three fastest-growing cities. During World War II, it was a centre for the construction of the Alaska Highway.

The discovery of oil at nearby Leduc, in 1947, began a new era of prosperity. The building of **refineries** and pipelines provided many jobs. Edmonton became the centre of oil refining and the **petrochemical industry** in western Canada.

Calgary

You read in chapter 2 that Jerry Potts was a guide for the North-West Mounted Police. In early 1875, Potts rode his horse to the spot where the Bow and the Elbow rivers meet. He chose this spot to build a new fort.

Later that year 50 men arrived with wagons full of supplies. They cut down trees and floated them down the Elbow River. They dug a trench and placed the logs upright to make a wall. By December they finished building the sleeping cabins, the stables for the horses, and a guardroom for prisoners.

At Christmas dinner, the officer in charge, Ephrem Brisebois, suggested that the fort be named for himself. His superior officer, James Macleod, turned down this bold request. Brisebois was not popular. Macleod named the new post Fort Calgary. No one knows for sure what "Calgary" means. It might mean "bay farm" in Macleod's home country of Scotland.

Unlike Edmonton, Fort Calgary was not an important fur trade post. It was a place where traders rested on their way to Fort Edmonton. The Canadian Pacific Railway, however, decided to make a railway route next to Fort Calgary. In August 1883 the railway arrived one kilometre away from Fort Calgary. Railway workers built a town site there and called it Calgary. Settlers rushed to buy land there. Some settlers moved their houses or stores from the fort to the new location.

New railways were built from Calgary to Edmonton, to Fort Macleod, and on to Lethbridge. Calgary became a busy place. It became a city in 1893. People brought cattle,

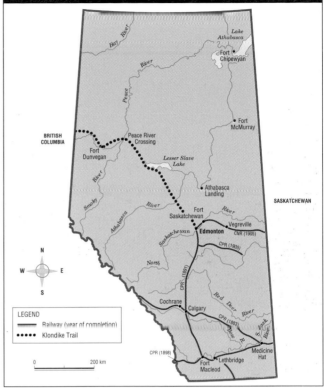

This map shows when the Canadian Pacific Railway (CPR) and the Canadian Northern Railway (CNR) reached parts of Alberta. It also shows the Klondike Trail, which was the route gold miners took to the Yukon.

People brought their goods to Calgary to ship to markets across Canada. These men are bringing furs from northern Alberta to Calgary for shipping in 1888.

READING MAPS

Study the map called "The Railway Comes to Alberta" on page 89. Answer the following questions.

1. When did the railway arrive in Calgary and Edmonton?
2. (a) What railway went through Calgary?

   (b) When were the railway routes through Calgary completed?

   (c) Explain why the railway was important to Calgary.
3. List the places that were on the Klondike Trail.

wheat, and coal to Calgary to ship to markets. In 1898 the CPR located its main freight yards in Calgary. The CPR parked and repaired some 700 railway cars in these yards. The yards provided jobs for more than 300 workers.

COW TOWN

One of Calgary's early success stories was Pat Burns. He began with a few cattle and ended up with a great fortune.

Burns made a lot of money by selling and shipping cattle to gold miners in the Yukon. They used the cattle for food. He owned ranches and built meat-packing plants in Calgary and six other cities. Meat-packing plants are places that prepare meat for shipping and selling at markets. He set up offices in countries all over the world.

OIL TOWN

In 1914 a new chapter opened in the history of Calgary. Oil was discovered only a few kilometres away, in Turner Valley. Since then Calgary has depended on oil and natural gas industries. Alberta's first oil refinery opened in Calgary in 1923.

More oil and gas were found at Turner Valley in the 1920s and 1930s. Calgary grew from a small prairie town to an important city in Canada.

Alberta in 1914

By 1914, Alberta had changed to look like the province we know today. Villages and towns had appeared among the prairie farms. The two cities of Calgary and Edmonton had passed all others in size and importance. They were already competing against each other.

By 1914, the railway connected most of Alberta's towns. Today, cars and airplanes have replaced the railway as a way to move people. The railway, however, is still important in moving Alberta's wheat, coal, and other products.

Wheat was still Alberta's most important product in 1914. However, anyone who travelled a few kilometres southwest of Calgary, to Turner Valley, would have seen the future in the oil wells on the landscape.

GATHERING INFORMATION

1. Explain the phrase, "The railway was as important to the life of the prairie as the sun or rain."
2. On a map of Alberta locate the first coal mines.
3. Why was coal mining such a dangerous occupation?
4. (a) When did the first discoveries of oil and gas take place?
   (b) Where was the largest and most important discovery of oil and gas located?
5. Explain the importance of oil and gas in Alberta's history.
6. Compare the growth of Edmonton and Calgary. How was their growth similar? How was it different?

FURTHER STUDY

1. Research the development of Edmonton and Calgary as cities. Explain how they competed historically and how they still compete today.
2. Edmonton has been described as "The Gateway to the North." Research why it has been described this way and make a presentation to the class. You may want to include the importance of the Klondike Gold Rush.
3. Find more information about Pat Burns. Write a paragraph describing how he was an important person in the history of Calgary.

1914 -1918 *World War I takes place*

1921 *United Farmers of Alberta form the government*

1919 *Union strikes in Edmonton and Calgary*

1933 *One in five workers in Canada are jobless*

1929 *The stock market crash in New York begins the Great Depression*

1935 *William Aberhart forms the first Social Credit government*

CHAPTER FOCUS

After World War I, farmers and workers organized to change Alberta. In the 1930s, all Albertans struggled to survive the Great Depression.

What was the Great Depression?

How did different groups organize to make life better for themselves?

How did World War I affect farmers and workers in Alberta?

What did people do to help one another?

CHAPTER 7

GROWING PAINS

Alberta was a busy new province. Many newcomers arrived in the first 10 years after Alberta became a province. Harvests were very good. New communities formed. The railway crossed the province.

After 1914, two world events brought great change to the lives of Albertans. These events were World War I and the Great Depression.

World War I

World War I began in 1914. Although the war was fought far away in Europe, it had a strong effect on Alberta.

When World War I began, many young Albertans rushed to join the army. They were eager to fight for the British Empire, although the war was very far away.

The soldiers hoped for a quick victory. But the war lasted for years. The war reduced the number of settlers coming from Europe. You read in chapter 4 that World War I caused some deep and bitter divisions among the people of Alberta.

The war, however, seemed to bring prosperity to farmers and workers. People began to farm more and more land because the price for wheat had increased. The farmers wanted to produce big crops to sell at high prices. There were also fewer workers. Workers could then ask to be paid more. Farmers borrowed large sums of money to buy more land and machinery, and to hire workers to help them.

When the war ended, the price of wheat dropped and jobs were hard to find. Soldiers who returned from the war could not find jobs. This made them angry because they felt they should be rewarded for fighting in the war. The soldiers also brought back a deadly disease called **influenza**. It spread through Alberta and killed more than 4000 people. The government ordered people to wear masks to protect themselves from disease.

In Alberta, 45 136 men joined the army during World War I. Of these men, 6140 died in the war.

The Farmers' Movement

The farmers of Alberta hoped that the dreams they had brought to Alberta would come true. They had built fine houses to replace their sod homes. They plowed the land and sold their crops.

Instead of getting an easier life, however, the farmers began to suffer hard times. They seemed unable to get out of **debt**. Alberta farmers depended mostly on growing one crop. That crop was wheat. They knew that all their hard work could be destroyed by frost or **drought**. Grain companies set the price that the farmers would receive for the wheat. The railway companies set the rate charged for moving the wheat to markets.

The farmers wanted to control their lives. They thought the banks and the railway charged too much money. They also wanted fairer prices for their grain. They wanted the government to help them, but it did not.

Henry Wise Wood and the United Farmers

Henry Wise Wood came to Alberta in 1905 from the United States. He settled on a farm in southern Alberta. He was a religious man who believed that people should co-operate, not compete. Wood helped the farmers organize into a group called the United Farmers of Alberta (UFA).

The UFA was a **social movement**. It was a group of farmers who organized to help each other. They believed they could co-operate and make life easier for one another.

THE FARMERS IN POLITICS

The UFA became a political party. The people of Alberta were tired of the old political parties, which were called the Liberals and the Conservatives. Albertans elected the UFA to be the government of Alberta in 1921.

This photograph shows members of the United Farmers of Alberta after they won the election in 1921. Why did the farmers in Alberta organize?

Herbert Greenfield was a farmer. He was born in England in 1867 and settled on a homestead north of Edmonton in 1906. When the UFA won the election, it asked him to become premier of Alberta. He was premier from 1921 to 1925.

John Edward Brownlee became the next premier. He was a lawyer who lived in Calgary. He worked for the United Farmers of Alberta and helped to organize the Alberta Wheat Pool. A wheat pool helps farmers sell their crops. In 1930, Brownlee had the Canadian government give Alberta control over its own land and natural resources.

Alberta Wheat Pool

In 1923 Alberta farmers formed the Alberta Wheat Pool to gain more control over the sale of their crops. The Pool collected the farmers' wheat, took it to market, and paid the farmers a fair price. The Pool then sold the wheat directly to foreign countries for the best possible price. If the Pool made a **profit**, the extra money was shared among the farmers.

The Workers Unite

Farmers organized to help each other by forming the UFA. Workers organized by forming **unions**. A union is a group of workers that tries to improve wages or working conditions. Wages are how much workers get paid. Working conditions include issues such as the number of hours a person has to work, and how safe the work area is.

Workers who joined unions included factory workers and coal miners. Many workers believed joining a union was the only

way to get fair treatment from their **employers**. These workers did not want to live in poverty anymore.

In the following account, a woman describes how being poor affected her family.

IN THEIR OWN WORDS

A Worker's Wife Describes Her Poverty

▼

"I find it practically impossible to dress our children and give them the education we feel they should have on the money my husband can earn. I, myself, if you will pardon me speaking personally, have taken my two eldest boys from school and put them to work simply because I could not afford to keep them at school.

There is no chance of a working man having a home to himself anymore as most of them have to take in roomers and boarders to eke out their incomes."

roomers and boarders - *people who pay to live and have meals at another person's house*
to eke out an income - *to struggle to make a living*

▲

The One Big Union

Workers became even more unhappy after World War I. Several union leaders met in Calgary in March 1919. They discussed how workers could make their employers pay a fair wage. These leaders made plans to join

Coal miners in Drumheller went on strike in 1919. They wanted their company to improve working conditions.

all unions together to form One Big Union (OBU). The OBU believed that they could make a world in which workers were treated fairly.

The most powerful weapon that a union has is the **strike**. In a strike, workers refuse to work until their employers give them better pay or better working conditions. Sometimes when workers go on strike, the employers try to meet their demands. Sometimes, however, the employers hire other people to replace the striking workers.

STRIKE IN DRUMHELLER

In 1919, the coal miners in Drumheller went on strike. They wanted their employer to make the mines safe to work in. Their employer replaced them with people who had just come back from fighting in World War I. These new workers attacked the miners and destroyed their houses. They chased the union leaders out of town.

GENERAL STRIKE

Most employers thought unions were bad for society. The employers asked the police for help during strikes. Sometimes the government used soldiers to stop strikes.

In 1919, union leaders asked workers in Winnipeg, Manitoba to hold a general strike. A general strike happens when all workers in a city go on strike. The Winnipeg General Strike ended with **riots**, and several leaders were put in jail.

In Calgary, about 1000 workers went on strike to support the Winnipeg General Strike. In Edmonton, 2000 workers went on strike too. This newspaper report describes what happened in Edmonton:

Streetcars, restaurants, a few businesses, closed down promptly at 11 o'clock . . . Electric power was shut off and water power decreased throughout the city.

The Changing World of the 1920s

The 1920s brought many changes to Alberta. Wheat prices went up and down. A long drought in southern Alberta caused many people to leave their farms. The important coal mining industry also became less prosperous. Although another 100 000 newcomers arrived in the late 1920s, even more left Alberta.

Changing Technology

The 1920s also brought new **technology**. Automobiles, radio, and movies came to Alberta in the 1920s. The automobile changed transportation. Radio and movies changed the way people amused themselves and the way they learned about the world.

Airplanes were another important change. Young Albertans who served in the air force during the war came home. They entertained people with airplane shows.

Wop May and Punch Dickins were famous bush pilots. A bush pilot is someone who flies a plane in the far north of Canada. They were two of the first pilots to move goods, people, and mail by plane. They explored northern Canada. They carried medicine to northern people.

UNDERSTANDING THE STORY

1. Conduct an interview with someone who lived during the Great Depression. (You may find someone from your family or from a senior citizens' home to interview.)
   (a) Read the descriptions of the Great Depression in this chapter. Use ideas from these descriptions to write questions to ask the person.
   (b) Be sure to ask the following questions:
      - How old were you during the Great Depression?
      - In what ways did the Great Depression change the way you lived?
2. Write down the person's answers to your questions. Present your interview to your class.

The Great Depression

October 24, 1929 was a day that changed Alberta for many years to come. On that day, so many people lost so much money on the **New York Stock Exchange** that the event was called the "Great Crash." This stock market crash affected the world. It began a time known as the Great Depression.

People lost a great deal of money in the crash. They could no longer afford to buy things. Many workers lost their jobs because businesses could not sell the goods they had made.

By 1933, at least one out of every five workers in Canada had lost their jobs. Unlike

IN THEIR OWN WORDS

A Worker Describes the Great Depression

▼

"Many . . . people here are without work and are in great need. Today a man called on me in despair. He has a wife and four children and he has only had two days work since January . . . They have had nothing in the house to eat. We have been keeping them in the bare necessities for some months. Today, I called on seven families in a similar plight."

despair - *being without hope*
bare necessities - *things needed to survive, such as food, water, clothing, and shelter*
called on - *visited*
plight - *a bad situation*

▲

Edmonton was not the only city in Alberta where jobless workers marched to ask for help from the government. This photograph shows people marching to the City Hall in Calgary in 1932.

today, there was no **unemployment insurance**. Workers without jobs could not get money from the government to survive. Some men moved from town to town looking for jobs. They rode in empty railway cars across Canada trying to find work.

The governments of Alberta and the cities did not have the money to help people who did not have jobs. These governments did, however, try to give money to families.

In the fall of 1932, two thousand jobless workers marched to the government building in Edmonton. They wanted to present a list of demands to the premier. They wanted help because they could not find work. They also wanted free medical care for when they were sick. This march led to violence between the marchers and the police.

Relief

In 1931, Canada did not have a good system of helping people without jobs. The government of Canada did not provide work for the jobless people across the country.

Governments within provinces and cities could give only a little help to families. This help was called "**relief**." For example, a family with three children received $60 a month from the government of Calgary. Thousands of families all over Alberta and eastern Canada were on relief.

There was no help at all, however, for unmarried men without a home. Finally, the government of Canada set up **relief camps** in 1932. These camps paid the men 20 cents a day for doing construction work in forested areas.

Ten relief camps were set up in Alberta. Most of the camps were set up in the foothills and mountain areas. Some camps were set up near Edmonton and Calgary. About 13 000 men worked in the camps in Alberta. They worked mainly on building highways. The men did not like the camps, which were run by the military. Some men described the camps as jails.

The writer James Gray describes in the following account how the men found some of the work to be useless.

IN THEIR OWN WORDS

James Gray Describes Work in a Relief Camp

▼

"We went out first with axes and cleared off the brush. Then we got picks and shovels and dug ditches. We threw the mud from the ditches into the road.

We levelled the road and graded it with hand tools. The job took the relief gangs all summer in 1932.

When we were finished, it was a nice mud road that started nowhere and for all I know, still leads to nowhere."

> **levelled and graded** - *made flat and even*
> **relief gangs** - *groups of men in the relief camp*

▲

The men disliked the relief camps so much that some went on strike. There were 19 strikes at relief camps in Alberta.

In April 1935, about 1500 men went on strike at relief camps in British Columbia. These men went to Vancouver to demand that the government close the camps. They also wanted to be paid fairly for the work that they had done.

At the end of May, these strikers decided to go to Ottawa to meet the Canadian prime minister and tell him their demands. These men rode empty railway cars on their journey to Ottawa. This event was called the "On-to-Ottawa Trek." They passed through Alberta on their journey.

Prime Minister R.B. Bennett decided that the trek must be stopped. The police in Regina tried to stop the trekkers when they came to that city. In the struggle, one police officer was killed, many men were hurt, and 130 people were arrested. The trek came to an end.

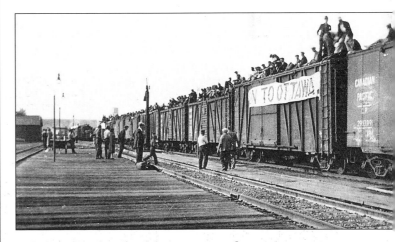

Thousands of jobless men rode empty railway cars on the "On-to-Ottawa Trek." Here, the men are at the railway station in Medicine Hat. Why were the men going to Ottawa?

The Dirty Thirties

The Great Depression was harder on the West than the rest of Canada. The price of wheat was the lowest in history. To make matters worse, many farmers had very little wheat to sell because of the bad weather. Drought dried out the soil and the hot prairie wind blew the soil away. Wild dust storms tore across the flat prairies of the West. Another name for the Great Depression was the Dirty Thirties.

The following account describes a dust storm in Hanna, Alberta.

IN THEIR OWN WORDS

A Farmer Describes a Dust Storm in Hanna

▼

"The morning is usually fine and clear, with maybe just a gentle breeze blowing . . . The breeze comes on just a little stronger, and a few small particles of soil start to drift gently along the top of the land . . . Very soon, with the increasing wind, the whole surface of the field is gently sifting along . . . There is nothing spectacular yet. But wait— away off to the northwest a heavy black cloud is forming between sky and earth. Black, yes, black as night. It sweeps towards us rapidly . . . and with a blast like a roar of a thousand lions it is upon us. We are alone in a sightless mass of hurtling soil, stinging sand and thumping clods."

> **sifting** - *moving*
> **hurtling** - *being thrown violently*
> **clods** - *lumps of soil*

▲

UNDERSTANDING THE STORY

Read the farmer's description of a dust storm.

1. In a group, write a story about a family on a farm watching a dust storm come in. Be sure to have the family members express their feelings about the storm and what will happen to their land. Perform the story in front of your class.

During the Great Depression, drought and wind blew valuable soil away. Dust storms gave the era the name the "Dirty Thirties."

Many farmers had borrowed money from banks to buy land or farm machines. But they could not afford to pay the banks back. Many banks took land and machines away from farmers because they could not pay. Many farmers wrote to Prime Minister Bennett to ask for help. One man from Mouse Mountain wrote the following letter in 1935:

IN THEIR OWN WORDS
A Letter to the Prime Minister

▼

"Dear Gentleman:
I am writing a letter to you explaining to you some of my dreadful misfortunes . . . I would like you to help me in some way. As now the times are hard, I cannot make a living in any way. Another horrible misfortune has occurred. On August thirteenth my house burned down, due to the striking of the lightning. Also the things that have been inside the house have burned down too. Now as I want to put up a new house I cannot get lumber because I have debts in many other places.
So now I live in the old granary. As winter is drawing nigh, I don't know how I am even going to get through it. Just recently on August fifteenth, we had a heavy frost here and ruined my crop. Now there is no possible way of making a living whatsoever . . . Please answer soon."

> **granary** - *a building where grain is stored*
> **nigh** - *near*

▲

The Bennett Buggy

During the Great Depression, many people could not afford to put gasoline in their automobiles. Some people hitched their cars to horses. The horses would pull the cars down the street. People called this form of transportation "Bennett Buggies," after

Prime Minister Bennett. They blamed Bennett for many of their problems. There is a picture of a Bennett Buggy on the timeline at the beginning of this chapter.

UNDERSTANDING THE PEOPLE

Read the section called "Social Credit."

1. Who was William Aberhart? What did he believe in?
2. Why did Albertans support Aberhart?
3. (a) What new technology did Aberhart use to reach Albertans?
   (b) Do people use technology to influence other people today? Explain.

Social Credit

For many people, the Great Depression caused the greatest upset in their lives. They had been raised to believe that if they worked hard, they would be rewarded with a better life for themselves and their families. Now millions of people could not find work no matter how hard they looked. Farmers could not sell their wheat. There was terrible poverty.

Major C.H. Douglas was an Englishman who believed he could help. He had an idea which he called "**Social Credit**." Businesses could not hire workers because no one could afford to buy their goods. Douglas's idea was for the government to give every person money. People could then buy goods, and businesses could hire workers.

William Aberhart was a preacher and school principal in Alberta. He liked the idea of giving people money. He used his radio show to tell other Albertans that social credit would rescue Canada from the Great Depression. Aberhart wanted to be premier of Alberta. He promised that if he was elected, every man, woman, and child in Alberta would receive $25.

In 1935 Aberhart's new Social Credit Party defeated the United Farmers of Alberta in the election. Although Aberhart made many changes to improve conditions, he was unable to pay the $25 he had promised.

Nevertheless, the Social Credit Party won 9 elections in a row and governed Alberta until 1971.

William Aberhart (left) and R.B. Bennett (right) shake hands. Aberhart was the premier of Alberta and Bennett was the prime minister of Canada during the Great Depression.

Lessons of the Great Depression

The Great Depression changed ideas about how the government worked. In 1935 Prime Minister Bennett's government set up the Canadian Wheat Board. The main purpose of this Board was to sell Canadian grain and to make sure that farmers received a certain price for wheat.

In 1940 Bennett's government also introduced unemployment insurance to give people money when they cannot find work. Today, the governments of Canada and Alberta still have these programs and many others to help people when times are bad.

Moving On

In this chapter, you learned that as Alberta grew, not all people shared the success. Farmers believed they were treated unfairly by railway and grain companies. Many workers believed that they were treated unfairly by their employers. Both of these groups tried to improve their lives by organizing.

The Great Depression in the 1930s brought poverty to many Albertans. The governments of Alberta and Canada had to think of ways to help the people. William Aberhart believed social credit was the answer.

Albertans continued to struggle through the Great Depression until another large event began: World War II.

GATHERING INFORMATION

1. How did World War I affect the growth of Alberta?
2. (a) What did the United Farmers of Alberta believe in?

    (b) What did the UFA do for Alberta's farmers?
3. Farmers in Alberta organized by forming the United Farmers of Alberta. How did workers organize? Explain.
4. (a) What caused the Great Depression?

    (b) The Great Depression was a time when many people could not find jobs. Why couldn't the governments of Alberta and its cities help the jobless workers?

    (c) How did the Great Depression change the lives of Albertans?
5. What changes did the government of Canada make because of the Great Depression?

FURTHER STUDY

1. Research how one of the following changed the lifestyles of Albertans:
    - automobiles
    - radio
    - movies
    - airplanes.

1939 *Indian Association of Alberta forms*

1942 *The United States begins building the Alaska Highway*

1939 *World War II begins*

1945 *World War II ends*

1942 *Japanese Canadians are put in internment camps*

1983 *The price of oil decreases*

1947 *Oil is discovered at Leduc*

CHAPTER FOCUS

In 1939, the Great Depression ended with the beginning of another major event: World War II. The war, and the oil boom and bust years that followed, brought more changes to the lives of Albertans.

There seems to be a lot of books about World War II. How did World War II affect people in Alberta?

What caused the oil boom in Alberta?

Does life get better for everyone during a "boom time?"

If Alberta has so much oil, why was there an oil bust in the 1980s?

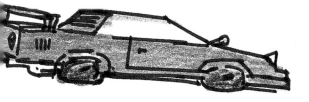

CHAPTER 8

BOOM AND BUST

World War II: 1939 to 1945

On September 10, 1939, Canada entered **World War II**. In this war, Germany, Italy, and Japan fought against Britain and its empire, France, the United States, the Soviet Union, and China.

The war turned Albertans' thoughts away from the Great Depression. Albertans joined the armed forces in large numbers. More than 78 000 men and 4500 women joined. While these men and women left Alberta to take part in the war, many other people came to live in Alberta.

The Air Training Plan

Canada became a place to train airplane pilots during the war. Alberta is a good place to fly airplanes. It has large areas of bright, open skies. There were 17 air bases in Alberta, where young men from all over the world learned to fly. These air bases changed life around nearby towns, such as Cold Lake and Wainwright.

MAX WARD

Max Ward was born in Edmonton. He taught pilots how to fly in World War II. After the war, he was a bush pilot. He carried supplies and passengers throughout northern Canada.

In 1953, Ward formed an airline company in Yellowknife. He called his company Wardair. He began flying supplies and passengers all over the world. Eventually, Ward moved his company to Edmonton. By 1975, Wardair was one of Canada's largest airline companies. Wardair was later bought by another airline company.

The Alaska Highway

The Japanese navy attacked Pearl Harbor in Hawaii in 1941. Americans were afraid that the Japanese would attack Alaska next. Alaska is the part of the United States that is located beside the Yukon. The Americans rushed to defend Alaska. They sent airplanes with supplies to Alaska. Many of these airplanes stopped at Edmonton. The war made Edmonton's airport the busiest in North America.

In 1942 the United States decided to build a highway through Canada to Alaska. More than 1400 American soldiers lived in Edmonton during the building of the Alaska Highway. This highway is still an important connection between Edmonton and northern Canada.

Max Ward flew a bush plane after World War II. He later started a successful airline company.

The War's Effect on the Farmers

World War II finally ended the Great Depression. Farmers in Alberta began getting higher prices for their wheat. They began to grow vegetables and sugar beets so that they would not have to depend on wheat only.

Farmers now could afford to buy more modern machines. More machines meant that farmers did not need as many workers as before to help harvest and do other chores. As a result, less than one-half of Albertans lived on farms by 1951.

Demand for Alberta's Coal

World War II also brought a new demand for Alberta's coal to fuel war ships and factories. As the war went on, more and more coal mines opened. At one time, some 8000 miners were working in 350 mines in Alberta. The government considered coal so important to the war that miners were not allowed to join the army. They had to stay in Alberta to mine coal.

This new interest in coal did not last after the war. After 1950 most Albertan homes used natural gas instead of coal. Natural gas was easier to use than coal. Coal had to be delivered by truck and shovelled into the furnace. But natural gas could be delivered to homes in a pipe.

Towns such as Drumheller, Lethbridge, and Nordegg were hurt by the loss of interest in coal. Some of the towns south of Drumheller disappeared.

By 1960 there were only about 1000 miners working in 100 mines in Alberta.

Alberta's coal was in demand because ships like these needed coal for fuel in World War II.

Enemies Within

War is the most serious and terrible human conflict. It creates fear and hatred. When war broke out with Germany, some Albertans were afraid that German Albertans would support their old country. Some Albertans whose sons or daughters were in the war were angry with those who did not go to war. They also turned their anger on the Hutterites, who were pacifists. They **persuaded** the government to stop the Hutterites from buying more land.

The Japanese Internment

During World War II, Canada was at war with Japan as well as Germany. Japan and British Columbia both have coasts along the Pacific Ocean. Many people in British Columbia were afraid that the Japanese would come across the ocean and attack them. These people wanted all Japanese people living in British Columbia to be removed from the coast. They were afraid that Japanese Canadians would help Japan.

As a result, some 22 000 Japanese were forced from their homes in British Columbia and put into **internment** camps. About 2600 Japanese were brought to Alberta where they were put to work on farms. The Japanese could not move from place to place without written permission.

Author Joy Kogawa was a child in British Columbia when the war began. Her family was forced to move to Coaldale, Alberta because they were originally from Japan. She tells her story in her book called *Obasan*.

IN THEIR OWN WORDS
Joy Kogawa Describes Her Feelings

▼

"We are leaving the BC coast – rain, cloud, mist – an air [full] of weeping. Behind us lies a salty sea within which swim our drowning specks of memory . . .

We are going down to the middle of the earth with pick-axe eyes . . . We are the chips and sand, the fragments of fragments that fly like arrows from the heart of the rock. We are the silences that speak from stone."

▲

UNDERSTANDING THE STORY

Read the description of Joy Kogawa's feelings.

1. Joy Kogawa expresses her sadness through powerful words. Choose one of the following expressions. Explain what Kogawa was trying to say with these words:

   (a) an air full of weeping
   (b) our drowning specks of memory
   (c) we are the chips and sand
   (d) we are the silences.

In 1988, Prime Minister Brian Mulroney apologized to the Japanese in Canada for their treatment during World War II. Every living Canadian relative of the Japanese who were moved in the war was paid $21 000.

Women During the War

With so many men in the army, large numbers of women went into the workplace. For many, it was the first time they were paid for working. Until then, most women in Alberta worked in the home or the farm. Now they worked in government, in factories, in meat-packing plants, and many other areas. They were paid less than men to do the same job.

In World War II, women did jobs that only men used to do. These women are building an airplane.

When the men returned home, most of the women went back into the homes. Still, women proved that they could work at "men's" jobs.

Native People During the War

Up to the 1940s, the Native people had gradually lost more and more control of their lives. The government sold some of their lands. They sent agents to the reserves to control the daily lives of the Native people. These agents had a lot of power. They did not let Native people perform their dances or ceremonies, or wear Native clothes.

The Schools

Many Canadians believed Native people had to become part of Canadian society to become successful. These Canadians believed that schools were the best place to make this change happen.

Native children were put into schools that were far away from their homes. The children were not allowed to speak their Native languages.

Natives Begin to Organize

During World War II, Native people began to organize as a group. They were led by three remarkable men. Malcolm Norris was a Metis. He devoted his life to improving the lives of Native people. John Callihoo was a Cree who had worked in the farmers' movement. John Laurie was a high school teacher in Calgary. He encouraged Native people to get an education.

These three men helped unite Native people who lived in far away areas of Alberta. They helped the Indian Association of Alberta to become a strong voice for Native people. This association helps Native people settle disagreements with the government of Alberta. These men urged the government to protect the rights of Native people.

Native people also gained more respect during World War II because they joined the armed forces in greater numbers than any other group. As a result, the government gave them more control over their own lives. For example, the government allowed them to perform Native ceremonies again.

JOHN CALLIHOO

John Callihoo was born on a Native reserve at Michel, Alberta. He was a farmer who was part Iroquois and part Cree.

During the 1930s, Callihoo helped to persuade the Alberta government to improve conditions for the Metis. He was nicknamed "the Lawyer" because he never gave up. He helped change the Indian Act to make it fairer. The Indian Act is a set of laws created by the government of Canada. These laws affect Native people. He also helped to strengthen the Indian Association of Alberta.

UNDERSTANDING THE PEOPLE

Read the information about John Callihoo.

1. Use the dictionary to find out what an association is. Ask three people you know if they belong to an association.
   (a) Ask them what association they belong to.
   (b) Ask them why they belong to an association.
   (c) Share your findings with your class.
2. Find out more about the Indian Association of Alberta. List some ways this association helps Native people to work together to improve their lives.

Oil Boom

An important discovery was made in Alberta after World War II ended. Around noon on February 13, 1947, oil was discovered in a farmer's field near Leduc. This is one of the dates to remember in the history of Alberta.

The discovery at Leduc caused Alberta's first oil **boom**. A boom is a time of sudden prosperity. Oil workers found more and more oil around Leduc. People who owned land there became wealthy.

Alberta's oil production increased from 7 million barrels in 1946 to 143 million barrels in 1956. A barrel is a unit that measures oil. One barrel is equal to 166 litres.

Oil completely changed the province of Alberta. It gave Alberta's government money to pay for new schools, universities, and

Why have some people called the discovery of oil at Leduc in 1947 the most important event in Alberta's history? Do you agree?

hospitals. It gave workers jobs. Oil companies needed many workers. The companies' offices in Calgary hired more geologists and more explorers. Many more workers got jobs building huge pipelines to carry the oil to Vancouver, to the United States, and to Ontario.

MAX BELL

Max Bell was born in Regina. In 1936, he borrowed $35 000 from friends and bought the *Calgary Albertan* newspaper. He became wealthy in the oil industry. He then bought many newspaper companies. More Canadians read his newspapers than any others.

Bell loved sports. He was one of the owners of the Vancouver Canucks hockey team. He also owned famous race horses.

Bell believed that fitness was very important. He often exercised during business meetings. At one meeting, he surprised everyone by walking across the room on his hands! He was 50 years old at the time.

 ## UNDERSTANDING THE PEOPLE

Read the descriptions of Eric Harvie and Max Bell.

1. Compare the lives of Eric Harvie and Max Bell. How did the oil boom affect their lives?
2. List the contributions these two men have made to Alberta.

ERIC HARVIE

Eric Harvie was born in Ontario and became a lawyer in Calgary. He owned land around Leduc and Redwater. When oil was found on his land, he became wealthy.

Harvie used his wealth to help museums. He set up the Glenbow Museum in Calgary. This museum is one of the largest in Alberta. He also helped the Calgary Zoo and the Banff Centre School of Fine Arts. He kept most of his good works a secret.

Oil Towns

The discovery of oil caused more towns to appear in Alberta.

During the fur trade, fur traders built posts along the rivers. When the railway came, settlers built towns around railway stations. When coal was successful, towns grew near coal mines. Now, towns were built near the oil and gas fields.

Some of these oil towns were brand new, like Swan Hills, Devon, Drayton Valley, and High Level. Other towns grew bigger, like Fort Saskatchewan, Red Deer, and Fort McMurray. Fort Saskatchewan became a centre of oil and gas refining. Red Deer also developed as a centre of oil and gas. Fort McMurray now had huge factories to turn oil sands into oil.

The oil industry made Calgary grow again. Hundreds of new companies opened their offices there. People in Calgary worked in banks that lent money to oil companies. Calgarians went to oil fields to drill for oil. They built equipment for workers to use. They sold workers food, fuel, and clothing.

The New Migration

The discovery of oil brought new wealth to Alberta. Good times attract newcomers, and many came to Alberta. The population of Alberta jumped from around 800 000 in 1946 to 1.3 million in 1961, and 2.2 million in 1981.

Many of the newcomers were **refugees**. They included people from India, Pakistan, and Ceylon. They also included new generations of Ukrainians, Russians, and Poles.

During the Great Migration, newcomers had settled on the land. They were farmers. After the oil boom, most newcomers came to

HOW MANY ALBERTANS LIVE ON FARMS?	
YEAR	PERCENTAGE OF ALBERTA'S POPULATION
1946	40%
1966	20%
1992	8% (approximately)

Why were fewer and fewer Albertans living on farms?

live in the cities of Alberta. Many people who lived on farms also moved to the cities to work.

Energy Crisis

Most of the oil in the world is produced in the *Middle East*. The Middle East is an area of southwestern Asia and northeastern Africa. Some countries in the Middle East include Saudi Arabia, Iran, and Iraq.

In 1973, the countries of the Middle East decided to raise the price of oil. This meant that people around the world had to pay more for gasoline, which is refined oil, and other oil products. People panicked. They formed long line-ups at gasoline stations to fill up their cars before prices went up. The high prices were a concern everywhere because most forms of transportation run on gasoline. Newspapers called this concern the Energy Crisis.

In Canada, the Energy Crisis caused conflict between Alberta and the Canadian government. Canadians depend on oil even more than most countries. They need it to heat their homes during the long winters. People in most Canadian provinces were worried about the rising cost of oil. In Alberta, however, people were pleased with the rising prices. Alberta would benefit from the high prices because it produced most of Canada's oil.

National Energy Program

The government of Canada decided to take action after the price of oil almost doubled again in 1979. Pierre Trudeau was the prime minister of Canada at the time. In 1980, he announced the creation of the National Energy Program (NEP).

The purpose of the National Energy Program was to protect Canadians from the rising price of oil. The program put new **taxes** on the sale of oil. These taxes were paid to the Canadian government in Ottawa. The Canadian government used the money from the taxes to create a new Canadian-owned oil company, called PetroCanada. The money was also used to buy oil from other countries so that the government could sell it to Canadians at a lower price. The NEP also made Alberta sell its oil to Canadians at a lower price.

Albertans were angry about the National Energy Program. Peter Lougheed was the premier of Alberta at the time. He was angry, too. He said that the Canadian government was taking away money that belonged to Alberta. He did not like how the taxes went to the Canadian government, instead of Alberta. He was also angry that Alberta had to sell its oil at a lower price.

Albertans argued that the oil in Alberta is a **non-renewable resource**. They wanted to save money to help Alberta when the oil ran out. They planned to help people set up businesses and develop other natural resources.

What did Peter Lougheed (left) and Pierre Trudeau (right) disagree about?

Peter Lougheed described the NEP as "the worst action ever taken . . . against a province in the entire history of Canada."

Lougheed believed this conflict was over more than just oil. He believed that Trudeau was trying to take away Alberta's control over its own affairs. In chapter 5, you read that Alberta had little control over its own affairs before it became a province. The Canadian government in Ottawa ran the territory. You also learned that Alberta was not given ownership of its natural resources until 1930. Lougheed believed Trudeau wanted the Canadian government to control Alberta again.

Lougheed threatened that Alberta would stop supplying oil to the rest of Canada if the province did not get a fair price. He had the province produce less oil. Many Albertans supported him.

In 1982, the price of oil began to decrease, and the NEP began to fall apart. After 1984, the new prime minister, Brian Mulroney, began to get rid of the program. The Energy Crisis, however, left a bitterness between Alberta and the government of Canada for many years after.

DISCUSSING THE ISSUES
WHO OWNS THE RESOURCES?

Activities

1. Do the following activities with a partner.
    (a) Choose one point of view expressed by these students. Have your partner choose a different point of view.
    (b) Defend the point of view you have chosen. Let your partner defend his or her point of view, too.
    (c) Discuss who you would have supported: Lougheed or Trudeau.

Oil Bust

In 1983, the price of oil around the world suddenly lowered. It decreased again in 1986 and stayed low into the 1990s. The low prices hurt Alberta. This was called an oil **bust**.

Lower oil prices meant less money for the province and fewer jobs for the workers. Many people left Alberta to look for jobs elsewhere. Once again, Albertans felt the weakness of relying on one natural resource. Farmers found that their wheat was not worth much in the Great Depression. In the same way, oil companies found that their oil was not worth much money in the 1980s.

During the great boom days of the 1970s, the Alberta government set up a savings fund to help when times are bad. By 1992, the savings were almost gone. Alberta struggled to overcome the oil bust.

GATHERING INFORMATION

1. How did Alberta participate in World War II?
2. Explain how World War II was good for Alberta's farmers.
3. When we apologize to someone, we usually are sorry for something we have done. Why did the Canadian government apologize to the Japanese Canadians in 1988?
4. Explain how the following natural resources have affected Alberta's history: furs, wheat, coal, and oil.
5. Explain how oil prices around the world affect Alberta.
6. Make a bar graph showing the number of Albertans who lived on farms in 1946, 1966, and 1992.

Booms and Busts

Throughout its history, Alberta has experienced several times of boom and bust. These kinds of changes have occurred in the rest of Canada, too. In Alberta, however, the booms and busts seem greater.

Historians suggest that booms and busts occur because Alberta has always depended too much on one resource. First there was fur, then wheat, then coal, and now oil. All these products are sold to the rest of the world. As a result, Albertans have no control over the price they receive for these products. For example, other countries may decide to sell their oil at a lower price than Alberta. Alberta then must lower its price to be able to sell its oil.

The government of Alberta has tried to help Albertans start other industries so that they will not depend so much on oil. Only time will tell if this will be successful, or if the future will bring more booms and busts.

FURTHER STUDY

1. Imagine you are a Japanese Canadian, Native person, or a farmer. Explain how World War II changed your life.
2. Do you think the Japanese Canadians and Native people were treated fairly during the war years? Prepare a debate to support your view. Try to imagine how people felt at that time.
3. Research what Alberta's oil industry is like today.
   (a) Are we in a time of boom or bust?
   (b) What could happen if a province depends on one or two natural resources for most of its wealth?

MAKING CONTRIBUTIONS

"While we read history, we make history."

History is being made every day. The things we do today will be looked on with interest many years from now. With a little imagination, we could put ourselves far into the future. We could try to explain how the computer, for example, changed the lives of Albertans in the 1990s. It might sound very much like the story of how the railway changed the lives of Albertans 100 years ago. Yet we are living these very changes today.

History can teach us how people in all ages deal with problems that still face us today. We can see, for example, how the meeting of Europeans and Native people changed the lives of both groups. In the fur trade days, the Native people and Europeans co-operated. The Native people provided the Europeans with valuable furs. The Native people showed them how to live off the land and how to move about by canoe. The Europeans brought new tools, guns, horses, cloth, and other things that changed the lives of the Native people.

When the bison disappeared and the Canadians wanted land for farming, the lives of Native people changed again. They lost their freedom and their way of life. Neither Europeans nor Native people understood how to deal with the problems they faced. Both groups are still trying to deal with these problems today. Each of us can help by trying to understand what happened in the past.

The Great Migration brought people to Alberta from all over the world. Each group brought its own skills and its own dreams. Each group has made its own contribution to Alberta. Many have kept the traditions of their former homes, which enrich the lives of all of us. From this experience, Alberta has built a society that accepts differences in people.

Albertans have grown the wheat, mined the coal, and drilled the oil. They have built towns and cities. They have lived through changes brought by World War I, the Great Depression, and World War II.

If we could hang the portraits of all the Albertans who have contributed to make the province, we would have a large and colourful gallery. Each of us could suggest his or her own list of wonderful people. Such a list might include a parent or grandparent who came to settle on a farm in Alberta, like Veronia Kokotailo or Ivan Pylypiw. It might include someone like John Ware, who overcame prejudice to become a successful rancher. It might include Native leaders like Red Crow and Crowfoot, who fought for the rights of their people. It might include political leaders such as Frank Oliver or Peter Lougheed. It might include leaders such as Emily Murphy, Nellie McClung, or Louise McKinney, who fought for the rights of women.

Every person has an important part to play in the making of history. Many of the things that we value most in our lives, such as freedom and co-operation, depend on our understanding of others. This understanding is the greatest contribution that any of us can make. It is a contribution we can make every day.

DISCUSSING THE ISSUES
MAKING A DIFFERENCE

Activities

You have now read many stories about people in Alberta's past.

1. (a) Look back in this book and choose three people whose stories interest you.

   (b) Explain why you think these three people are interesting.

   (c) Describe how these three people made a contribution to Alberta's past.

2. Read today's newspaper or listen to the news on the radio. Describe people who you think are contributing to history.

GLOSSARY

A

Adapted means to have changed to meet new conditions.

Agents are people who act for others. For example, agents acted for the railway to advertise the western lands in Canada.

Ancestors are family relations of long ago, for example, the grandparents of your grandparents.

Archaeologists study the remains of tools, houses, monuments, and other things left by people who lived long ago.

Asia is the largest continent. It is the land of origin of the first people.

An **association** is a group of people organized to perform a certain task or to accomplish a certain goal.

Attitudes are ways of thinking.

The **Austrian Empire** was a large area of Eastern Europe ruled by Austria. It included many different groups of people, such as Ukrainians and Romanians.

An **awl** is a small, pointed tool used for drilling holes.

B

Babiche is made of strips of leather made from bison or deer hide. It is used for laces or thread.

Bands are groups of Native people who lived together in a certain area.

Bees are social gatherings in which people work together to help their neighbour build a barn or house or make a quilt. Work is usually mixed with eating and fun.

A **bluff** is a steep hill or cliff, usually at the edge of a river, lake, or sea.

A **boom** is a sudden period of prosperity.

Boundaries are lines that separate areas, such as farms, provinces, or countries.

Branded is marked by a brand. For example, cattle are marked with a hot iron to show who owns them.

The **British** are the people of Britain. Britain is made up of England, Scotland, Wales, and Northern Ireland.

The **British Empire** was the world-wide collection of countries, including Canada, that was controlled by Britain.

The **British North America Act** is the legislation that allowed Nova Scotia, New Brunswick, Ontario, and Quebec to join to become Canada in 1867.

Buffalo jumps are places where the Native people drove bison over a cliff.

A **bust** is the sudden end of a time of prosperity.

C

A **capital city** is a town or city where the government of a country or province meets. Edmonton is the capital city of Alberta.

A **Catholic** is a member of the Roman Catholic Church.

A **charm** is an object that a person believes has magical powers.

Chinooks are moist, warm winds blowing from the Pacific Ocean, across the eastern slopes of the Rocky Mountains and into Alberta. Chinooks cause a rapid rise in temperature.

Climate is the weather conditions, such as temperature and rainfall, over a long period of time.

A **community** is a group of people with common interests or origins.

Competition is a contest between two people or groups in which each side tries to do better than the other.

Conflict is a struggle or fight between people or groups with different beliefs or ideas.

A **constitution** is the written law of a country such as Canada.

Co-operated means worked together towards a certain goal.

Culture is a term used to describe the beliefs, customs, and arts of a certain people.

Customs are practices followed by habit among a group of people.

D

Debt is what is owed, usually money.

Dene means "the people." The Dene are the Athapaskan-speaking peoples of the Northwest Territories today.

Descendants are the children and grandchildren of certain people.

Desolate means lonely and unhappy.

Discrimination is an act that denies a person's rights or peace.

Dreamers are Native people who believe they can tell the future through dreams.

Drought is a long time with no rain.

E

Electing is choosing by voting.

Employers are people who pay others (called employees) to work.

Energy is the potential of something to do work. We can use natural resources such as wind, water, coal, electricity, and petroleum to do work for us. Energy also refers to heat or electric power that we can use.

An **English Lord** is a man of high rank in Britain. A Lord passes his rank to one of his sons after his death. A Lord's wife has the rank of Lady.

Enterprising is full of energy and imagination.

Equal means having the same rights as others.

An **estate** is property or land, usually of considerable size.

F

Fare is the price a passenger pays to ride a train, ship, or other means of transportation.

Fast means to stop eating for a time, especially as part of a religious activity.

Ferries are boats used to move people and goods across a body of water.

Founded means set up or begun.

Fringes are threads or cords that decorate the edges of clothing

Fuel is material such as coal or oil burned to produce light or heat.

Furrows are long, narrow cuts in the ground in which a farmer plants seeds.

G

A **generation** is all the people born at about the same time. Your parents belong to one generation, and you belong to the next generation.

Geologists are people who study the origin, history, and structure of the earth.

Glaciers are huge sheets of ice.

The **governor general** is the representative of the British king or queen in Canada.

To **graze** is to eat growing grass. For example, cattle graze in a field.

The **Great Migration** is the time from 1896 to 1921 when large numbers of newcomers came to Canada.

A **grist mill** grinds grain into flour. Grist is grain ready for grinding.

Guides are people who show others the way by leading them or pointing out directions.

H

A **habitation** is a house or shack.

Harmony is agreement, friendship, and peace.

Hides are animal skins used to make clothing or covers.

An **historian** is a person who studies the past.

History refers to things that happened in past time. It also refers to the study of past time.

Homesteads are lands claimed by settlers. To homestead is to settle and farm land.

Hot springs are natural springs of hot water.

Hudson's Bay Company is a company formed by Europeans at Hudson Bay in 1670. The purpose of the company was to trade goods for furs with the Native people. At first, Native people had to make long, dangerous journeys to Hudson Bay to trade. Later, the company built trading posts on rivers in the West. The Natives then did not have to travel so far. Today, the company is a department store called "The Bay."

I

Immigrants are people who leave their country of origin to live in another country.

Industry is the production and sale of goods and services.

Inferior means something is less worthy or important than something else.

Influenza is a disease that results in fever, muscle pain, and sometimes death.

Inherit means to receive property from another person after he or she dies.

Internment is to be put in prison, especially during a war.

Isolated means separated from other people.

K

The **Klondike Gold Rush** was the dash of thousands of gold-seekers to the Yukon. It began in 1897 and was named for Klondike Creek, where gold was first discovered. Many of the gold-seekers passed through Edmonton on their way north. They bought food and clothing there for the long and dangerous trip through the forests and mountains.

L

Leased is to have been sold or given the use of land.

Leggings are coverings for the legs worn by the Native people.

A **luxury** is something that costs a lot of money. A luxury is enjoyable but is not necessary.

M

A **majority** is the largest part of a group.

Manitou is the name of the Great Spirit.

A **medicine bundle** is a small bag made of animal skin used by Native people to hold items that were special to them. The bundle could only be opened at certain times and shown to certain people.

Medicine wheels are monuments of stones left by the Plains people. These stones are placed in a pattern that resembles the spokes of a wheel.

A **Metis** is a person of mixed European and Native origin.

Missions are districts or local churches served by priests.

Moldy means covered with a furry fungus.

Monuments are structures built to celebrate an event, such as a victory in war or the passing of a season.

Myths are stories passed from generation to generation. Most myths try to explain why things came to be as they are today.

N

A **National Park** is an area of land set aside by the government of Canada to preserve the wildlife and natural beauty.

Natural resources are materials found in nature that are necessary or useful to people. Coal, oil, forests, and water are examples of natural resources.

The **New York Stock Exchange** is the place in the city of New York where stocks are bought and sold. A stock exchange is also called a stock market. Stocks are shares of a company which are sold to the general public. If the company does well, its shares rise and those who own shares receive money. If the company fails, the shares become worthless.

Nomadic means wandering from place to place, usually in search of food.

A **non-renewable resource** is a natural resource that cannot be replaced once it is removed. Oil is an example of a non-renewable resource.

O

An **organization** is a group of people who meet and act together to achieve a certain purpose.

Origin refers to who one's parents are. Origin can also refer to the place from which someone comes.

P

The **Palliser Triangle** is a large section of land in southern Alberta that John Palliser thought was a desert. A desert cannot be used as farmland.

Pamphlets are folded pieces of paper with information printed on them. They are printed in large numbers and passed around to inform people.

A **patron saint** is a saint who gives special protection to an individual or a group. A saint is a very holy person who can help people on Earth.

To **persuade** is to use reason and argument to change someone else's feelings or opinion.

The **petrochemical industry** is the industry in which products are made from petroleum. Plastics are an example of these products.

Pipelines are pipes used to move liquid or gas, such as oil or natural gas.

Plains are the flat or rolling grasslands of western Canada. They are also called prairies.

A **policy** is the plan of action of a government.

Political parties are organizations of people with similar political views and goals.

Poverty is the state of not being able to afford adequate food and housing.

Prejudice is an unreasonable opinion that leads to suspicion or hatred of a particular group of people.

Prestige is the quality of being admired.

Profit is money left over when a business makes more money than it spends.

Promised land is a place of happiness. In the *Bible* the Promised Land was the land that God promised to the Jews.

Prospects are chances of success.

To be **prosperous** is to have success and to be well-off.

A **Protestant** is a member of any of the Christian churches that separated from the Roman Catholic Church.

Provinces are separate territories within Canada that have their own governments. Canada has ten provinces.

Q

Quartzite is a hard rock found in sandstone and granite.

Quests are Native ceremonies in which a person looks for guidance from the spirit world.

R

Race is a division of human beings according to the colour of their skin or some other physical characteristic.

Racism is the opinion that one's own group is better than others.

Ranchers are people who raise cattle.

Ranked means arranged in order of importance.

Rates are the cost for each unit of a good or service, such as the rate to ship a certain amount of wheat by train.

Refineries are places where oil is made into gasoline and other products.

Refugees are people who leave their native land because they are being treated badly for political or religious reasons.

Relief is money received from the government because of need or poverty.

Relief camps were places set up during the Great Depression to house unemployed people.

Religious ceremonies are a set of acts performed to honour or to contact gods or spirits.

A **reserve** is land set aside for use by Native people.

Rights are that which is owing to someone by law or tradition. Rights are what is fair.

Riots are violent outbursts by a group of people.

A **rodeo** is a competition in which cowboys compete in events such as riding wild horses or roping cattle.

Romantic means that which is appealing to the imagination.

Round-up means to gather cattle together from various places.

S

A **sawmill** is a place where lumber is cut into boards by a machine.

A **scandal** is an act by those in government that brings about disgrace.

A **scene** is a picture or an image.

Sections are units of land. One section is equal to 256 hectares. There were 36 sections in a township.

The **Senate** is a division of the government of Canada.

A **shaman** is sometimes called a medicine man. A shaman is a Native person with special healing powers.

Sheaves are a bundle of grain bound with straw or string.

A **shift** is the time when a group of workers is required to work.

A **shingled** roof is covered with flat pieces of wood called shingles.

A **sickle** is a farm tool with a blade attached to a short handle. It is used for cutting grain or tall grass.

Sinew is a tough, stringy part of an animal used by the Native people as thread or string.

A **slave** is a person who is owned and treated like property. A slave must work for his or her owner and could be sold to another owner.

Slavery is the custom of owning slaves. Many white people owned Black slaves in the United States before 1865.

Smallpox is a serious, often deadly, disease marked by high fever and a severe skin rash. It is caused by a virus. It killed many Native people. Today the disease is very rare because of vaccination.

Social Credit was an economic plan to give every citizen money to buy goods in order to raise society out of the Great Depression. The Social Credit Party was founded on this plan.

A **social group** is a number of people who share a common origin or interest or characteristic.

A **social movement** is the activities of a group of people towards achieving a specific goal.

A **society** is all the people of a particular place who share customs and activities.

A **spring** is a natural flow of water from an underground stream.

Stampeding refers to a herd of animals, such as bison or cattle, running suddenly.

Stocks are the main stem of plants.

A **storehouse** is a place where food, clothing, and other things are kept.

A **strike** is a stopping of work by employees to demand for higher pay or better working conditions.

Sugar beet is a vegetable from which sugar is made.

Sulphur is a pale-yellow substance used to make gunpowder, matches, and some medicines.

Superior means greater than. Superior is the opposite of inferior.

Surveyors are people who measure and map the land.

Symbols are marks or objects which have special meanings.

T

Taxes are money paid to support a government.

Technology is the use of science in practical ways. It involves using materials, tools, machines, and methods to produce goods and services.

The **telegraph** is a means of communication that sends and receives simple electric messages, called telegrams.

Tipis are dwellings used by Native people. The Plains people used bison hides stretched over tent poles. The Woodland groups used bark as a covering.

Title is the ownership of land. It also means the paper on which this ownership is spelled out.

Tradespeople are skilled workers, such as miners or carpenters.

Traditions are beliefs or customs handed down from one generation to the next.

A **travois** was a kind of trailer used by Plains people. It consisted of two long poles that were placed over the shoulders of a dog or horse.

Treason is the act of betraying one's country or ruler.

Treaties are agreements between the leaders of two peoples or governments. In Canada, Native people signed agreements with the government of Canada.

Treaty Number 7 was an agreement signed in 1877 by the Canadian government and the Peigan, Blackfoot, Blood, and Sarcee. These Native peoples gave up their rights to land in southern Alberta in return for parcels of land called reserves.

Treaty Number 8 was an agreement signed in 1899 by the Canadian government and the Cree, Chipewyan, Beaver, and Slavey. These Native peoples gave up their rights to northern Alberta, northwestern Saskatchewan, and northeastern British Columbia in return for parcels of land called reserves.

Tumplines are headbands used to support heavy loads.

U

Unemployment insurance is money paid to workers when they lose their jobs.

The **Union Jack** is the flag of Britain.

Unions are organizations whose goal is to improve the wages and working conditions of workers.

V

A **vision** is an image created by the imagination. To Native people, a vision is the experience of seeing the future through the eyes of a spirit.

Voyageurs were the men who paddled and carried the canoes used in the fur trade. Most voyageurs were French Canadians or Metis.

W

A **witness** is a someone who was present when something happened.

Woodlands are areas covered with trees, like northern Alberta.

A **woolly mammoth** is a large, shaggy elephant that once lived in North America and Europe. It stood about 4.1 m high at the shoulder.

World War I was a war fought from 1914 to 1918. Britain, Canada, France, Russia, Belgium, Italy, Japan, the United States, and others fought against Germany, Austria-Hungary, Turkey, and Bulgaria.

World War II was a war fought from 1939 to 1945. Britain and its empire (including Canada), France, the United States, the Soviet Union, and China fought against Germany, Italy, and Japan.

INDEX